TWAYNE'S WORLD AUTHORS SERIES

A Survey of the World's Literature

Sylvia E. Bowman, Indiana University

GENERAL EDITOR

SOUTH AFRICA

Joseph Jones, University of Texas

EDITOR

Francis Carey Slater

(*TWAS 173*)

TWAYNE'S WORLD AUTHORS SERIES (TWAS)

The purpose of TWAS is to survey the major writers— novelists, dramatists, historians, poets, philosophers, and critics—of the nations of the world. Among the national literatures covered are those of Australia, Canada, China, Eastern Europe, France, Germany, Greece, India, Italy, Japan, Latin America, New Zealand, Poland, Russia, Scandinavia, Spain, and the African nations, as well as Hebrew, Yiddish, and Latin Classical literatures. This survey is complemented by Twayne's United States Authors Series and English Authors Series.

The intent of each volume in these series is to present a critical-analytical study of the works of the writer; to include biographical and historical material that may be necessary for understanding, appreciation, and critical appraisal of the writer; and to present all material in clear, concise English—but not to vitiate the scholarly content of the work by doing so.

Francis Carey Slater

By JOHN ROBERT DOYLE, JR.

The Citadel

Twayne Publishers, Inc.   ::   New York

For My Sisters
Thelma and Louise

Preface

THIS BOOK had its inception in a lecture trip to the Eastern Cape. An early morning flight from Johannesburg had taken me into and out of Durban on time. The plane, scheduled to land at East London, was flying south at about five thousand feet over water and giving passengers on the west side a perfect view of the Natal coast. All was going well. The wheels were down and almost on the field at East London. Suddenly I noticed the wing controls shift, and the plane shot back into the air. Soon the captain explained that a forty-mile cross wind had blown off the Indian Ocean, and since there was only one landing strip not undergoing repairs at East London he was flying on to Port Elizabeth. In fifty minutes we were on the ground, but it required seventeen hours for me to return by train to the point of my lecture engagement at the University College of Fort Hare.

It was in 1820 that Francis Carey Slater's great-grandparents started from Port Elizabeth. To them my pace inland would have seemed magically rapid, but to me it was so slow that I had a chance to observe in detail the country through which I passed. Climbing the hills as we approached Slater's beloved Alice, the train dropped to a speed which tempted a person to get out and walk beside it. Looking back, I agree that the important fact was the *lack* of speed.

Now followed a visit in the Alice-Lovedale vicinity. There was the Amatola range, especially Hogsback to be climbed, and the whole country to be absorbed. I was taken into the Xhosa area, to a native trading post, and to a vegetable auction market. All of this presents the country from which the "Dark Folk" pieces came. A high percentage of the student body at Fort Hare is Xhosa; I had a chance to meet them in small groups, and some of the gatherings quite informal. This brought me close to students of the type Slater had known at Lovedale—allowing, of course, for the time difference.

Other trips about South Africa put me in touch with almost every area about which Slater speaks, including the Drakensberg and the Karroo. Finally, settled in Cape Town, I was only a fraction of a mile from the home in which Slater lived for twenty-five years, after his retirement as a bank manager in Grahamstown.

The present volume follows a study of the poems, stories, novels, and other work of William Plomer, born in Pietersburg, the Transvaal, during the time Slater was in the bank at Matatiele. As the very young Plomer was publishing his first poems, stories, and a novel, Slater was nearing retirement from the bank and ready to do his best work. Taken together, these two men represent a considerable span of South African literature in English. It should be remarked that to examine the writing of these two turns essentially into a study in contrast.

J. R. D., Jr.

The Citadel
Charleston, South Carolina

Acknowledgments

The author offers grateful acknowledgment to the following for permission to quote from various books.

To William Blackwood & Sons Ltd. for permission to quote from *Footpaths Thro' the Veld, From Mimosa Land, Calls Across the Sea, Settlers and Sunbirds, The Karroo and Other Poems, Drought, Dark Folk and Other Poems, The Trek, Veld Patriarch,* and *Collected Poems.*

To Longmans Green & Co. Ltd. for permission to quote from *The Shining River, The Centenary Book of South African Verse,* and *Veld Patriarch.*

To the Lovedale Press for permission to quote from *Settlers' Heritage.*

To Digby, Long & Co. for permission to quote from *The Sunburnt South.*

To Nash and Grayson for permission to quote from *The Secret Veld.*

To the Oxford Press for permission to quote "To the Veld," by Arthur Shearly Cripps.

To David Nutt for permission to quote "Burial," by Kingsley Fairbridge.

To A. A. Balkema for permission to quote from *A Critical Survey of South African Poetry in English.*

I offer my very special appreciation to Professor R. G. Howarth, head of The Department of Literature, University of Cape Town, and to Dr. A. M. Lewin Robinson, Director of the South African Public Library, who saw to it that I received the excellent picture of Francis Carey Slater used on the dustjacket of this book. Credit for this photograph goes to *The Cape Argus* along with my sincere thanks for its use.

Any deficiencies in the bibliography of this book must be my responsibility, but its admirable thoroughness is the result of the meticulous research of Mr. Dudley Horner, the Library School of the University of the Witwatersrand, Johannesburg. Mr. Horner has furnished me with far more material than could be printed in a Selected Bibliography.

Contents

Chronology

1876   Francis Carey Slater was born August 15, at Umjilo, a farm about three miles from Alice, in the Eastern Cape.

1880   In May the Slater family left Umjilo for Brakfontein, about seventeen miles from Alice.

1887   Attended the Queen's Jubilee in Grahamstown.

1891   Two brothers, Ernest and Charles, died in January. During March, Francis, aged fourteen, started his formal schooling at Lovedale.

1893   In July, within one month of his seventeenth birthday, he went to work in Alice as a bookkeeper for Baker King and Co.

1894   Towards the end of the year, Dr. and Mrs. James Stewart and six of their children returned to Lovedale from abroad.

1895   Gave a paper on Charles Tennyson-Turner at the Alice Literary Society.

1896   Gave a paper on "The Poetry of South Africa" at the Alice Literary Society.

1897   Attended the Queen's Diamond Jubilee in Grahamstown.

1898   Sir Alfred (later Lord) Milner visited Lovedale.

1899   In January, Slater resigned from his job in Alice and spent several months at home. In April went to Port Elizabeth looking for work and found a place with the Standard Bank of South Africa. After five months with the Port Elizabeth branch of the Standard Bank, was sent to East London.

1900   Toward the middle of the year, was sent by the bank with cash to pay the troops through a branch bank at Aliwal North.

1901   In December was appointed acting accountant of the branch at Matatiele in East Guiqueland.

1902   Death of father.

1905   When long leave came, departed in April for his first visit to England and Europe, taking with him the poems which were to make up his first book, *Footpaths Thro' the Veld*.

1906   Sent temporarily as a clerk to the Grahamstown branch of the Standard Bank.

1907   In February sent as accountant to the Graaff-Reinet branch. Went for three months as manager of the Naauwpoort bank and then was made accountant at Dordrecht. Seven of his poems published in *A Treasury of South African Poetry and Verse*, edited by E. H. Crouch.

1908   Published a collection of his stories entitled *The Sunburnt South*, written in six months while at Dordrecht, where he remained for slightly more than two years.

1910   In February was made accountant at Somerset East. The third week in May was sent as acting manager for a new branch at Alexandria and after three weeks transferred to start a new branch at Peddie. On September 29 married Leonora Nyassa Stewart, the third daughter of Dr. and Mrs. Stewart of Lovedale. Near the end of the year *From Mimosa Land* was published.

1913   Sent to relieve the manager of the branch at Barkly East.

1916   Another volume of verse, *Calls Across the Sea*, published with a 1917 date on the title page.

1917   In December was promoted to the management of the Grahamstown branch of the Standard Bank. Here he remained twelve years, until his retirement.

1919   Published another volume of verse, *Settlers and Sunbirds*.

1920   He and his wife visited England and Scotland.

1924   *The Karroo and Other Poems* published.

1925   *The Shining River*, his only novel, published, and he selected and edited *The Centenary Book of South African Verse*. He and his wife visited England, Scotland, and the Western Isles.

1929   Under the pseudonym Jan Van Avond published *Drought, A South African Parable*.

1930   When long leave came, he requested that he be allowed to retire at the end of the period, just before his fifty-fifth birthday. His request was granted, and he and his wife left for a trip to England. He returned to South Africa early in 1931, following the death of his mother.

1931   Moved from the eastern Province to Cape Town.

1933   Visited Victoria Falls, the Matoppos, and the Zimbabwe Ruins.

1934   Went to England and then on to the Continent, making visits to Paris, Geneva, Milan, Venice, Florence, Pisa, Rome, Naples, Bari, Athens, Corinth, Corfu, Cattaro, Ragusa or Dubrovnik, Belgrade, Budapest, Vienna, Prague, Brussels.

1935   *Dark Folk and Other Poems* published.
1936   Began a study of materials to be used in *The Trek*.
1938   *The Trek* published. Trip to England and Norway.
1939   Between 1939 and 1944 Slater suffered several severe illnesses.
1941   *The Distraught Airman* published.
1944   Set to work on a revised edition of the *Centenary Book of South African Verse*.
1945   *The New Centenary Book of South African Verse* published.
1947   In May *Selected Poems* published. Given an honorary D.Litt. from the University of South Africa.
1949   *Veld Patriarch and Other Poems* published. Made a voyage around the East Coast to Beira, Umtali, Salisbury. Visited Arthur Shearly Cripps, a poet he had long admired.
1954   *Settlers' Heritage*, an autobiography, published at Lovedale.
1957   *Collected Poems* published.
1958   Leonora Nyassa Slater died, July 15. Francis Carey Slater died in Cape Town, September 2.

CHAPTER 1

Beginnings

P UTTING into Algoa Bay, Eastern Cape, with British Settlers of 1820, the sailing ship *Aurora* brought to South Africa four great-grandparents of Francis Carey Slater. The paternal great-grandfather, Thomas Slater, was a man of independent means, scholarly, and with some competence as an amateur artist. He had made the long voyage for neither adventure or gain, but because his physician had advised a warmer climate. To him and his family the South African sun beckoned, and he followed its rays. As with other settlers, the Slaters moved inland and with several families formed what was to become the village of Salem, some fourteen miles southwest of Grahamstown. With assistance from their father, two of the Slater sons became successful businessmen and two farmers and landowners. One of the business sons and one farmer served in the Legislative Assembly, now Parliament. Thomas Slater himself, despite the requirements of a pioneer life, continued to read books and to paint a few pictures, some of the spirit of a gentle life being retained in this new and very raw situation.[1]

Aboard the same ship that brought the Slaters were Joseph Edward Wilmot and his wife, Ann, who became the maternal great-grandparents of Francis Carey Slater. In control of considerable income from England, Wilmot was able to purchase several farms, the largest of which was passed on to his son, John Richmond, who became the author's grandfather. This particular farm was at Springvale, thirty-five miles from Grahamstown. John Wilmot was spoken of by his daughter, Alicia, the author's mother, as a man who cared for books and was kindly, gentle, and religious. In his autobiography, Francis Carey, with obvious pleasure, recalls visits to Springvale.

I *Birth and Childhood*

When Francis was born, August 15, 1876, his parents were

15

living at Umjilo, a farm about three miles from Alice, whose mission school, Lovedale, was to be very important in the boy's life. In May, 1880 the family moved to Brakfontein, a three-thousand-acre farm beside the Keiskama River, about seventeen miles from Alice and forty-seven from Grahamstown. Here there was one close English neighbor, but the other near neighbors were Afrikaners. Thus, for natural reasons rather than because of instruction, Francis spoke Afrikaans along with Xhosa and English.

As a child Francis seems to have had a great fondness for his grandmother Wilmot, who according to his account showed the child very special attention during family visits to Springvale. Grandmother Wilmot was the only source of Scottish blood in the family; otherwise the author-to-be was totally English. At least in this generation, the girls dominated the family, and Francis reports that there were nine aunts—all handsome, accomplished housekeepers, who wrote good hands and could spell—and all married.

Upon these family visits some days were spent with the Wilmots and then the family would move on to Grandmother Slater's, about fifteen miles beyond Springvale. Grandfather Slater had died a few days before Francis was born, but his widow had assumed management of his estate. The Slater family offered young Francis six aunts and five uncles. The girls were said to be good looking, intelligent, and for the period, well-educated—though only one married. Of the six, Frances Charlotte, as "Francis Bancroft," became a popular novelist. These intellectually inclined aunts seem to have used family visits as a time for schooling their nieces and nephews.

At the Slaters' lived his father's oldest sister, always spoken of as "Old Aunt," who attained the age of a hundred and two. She was already in her late eighties when Francis first knew her. Though of independent means, for many years in Grahamstown "Old Aunt" had conducted a boarding school for girls, finally retiring to her brother's farm, where Francis had known her.

II   *Early Reading and Development*

Though the education of Francis was not systematic, it appears to have been successful. His mother and father did what they could with reading, spelling, and arithmetic. A visiting aunt always became a teacher. From one source or another, the boy learned, and

when he reached six started out to read anything he was permitted
to have. Now his mind began to be filled with influences that for
seventy years would guide his life. Francis was eight when his
father returned one day from Grahamstown with a parcel containing
the poems and plays of William Shakespeare and the poetical works
of Milton, Wordsworth, Scott, Burns, and Longfellow. It was Scott's
narrative quality which appealed first to the exploring young reader;
then came an interest in rhythm and rhyme. An introduction to
Shakespeare developed through reading by his parents in the even-
ings. Next the boy sampled Wordsworth, then Longfellow. Burns
followed, but Milton was too much for the eight-year-old. He per-
sisted, however, and had read *Paradise Lost* by the age of ten. In
his ninth year he bought with his own money, eighteen pence, his
first book, a small copy of Byron's poems. Also during his ninth
year, he began to borrow volumes from a minister who had moved
from Alice to a home about two miles from the Slaters. For the growing boy, the minister's conversation was probably as important as
his books. During the next year there came to this neighborhood
another family, some eight miles distant, which was to have a
profound effect upon the literary-minded youth. This family
loaned Francis all of the Scott novels, starting with *Rob Roy* and
then *Ivanhoe.* Thus, between the ages of ten and twelve, he was
introduced to the fictional world of a congenial author. In his
eleventh year Francis read his first Dickens and became an admirer
of Oliver Schreiner's *Story of an African Farm.* A little later he read
all of Tennyson, including the plays. Apparently as a practical joke,
one of his father's friends loaned him Adam Smith's *Wealth of
Nations.* He also came upon Keats, Shelley, and Coleridge.

Even a voracious reader need not have a desire to write, but
Francis Carey Slater very early seems to have developed literary
inclinations. His initial attempt at verse came in his eighth year.
This is a rather usual time for first efforts, but once he started
Francis appears never to have stopped. By the age of twelve or
thirteen, he was attempting sonnets. At fourteen he wrote an
eighty-seven-line poem using terza-rima. From the age of eight
he not only began to compose but to notice the South African environment which was to become the basis for much he was to write.
He observed and also became aware that he was observing. Deeply
moved by the sight of the Amatola Mountains, he later mentioned
viewing them in an attitude of youthful worship. He explored the

country around him and became familiar with rocks, trees, flowers
—the whole of the natural world—in intimate detail. He also made
the human world a dominant part of his consciousness. The native
Xhosas he knew—their language, attitudes, stories. Likewise, the
Afrikaner neighbors were very much a part of his life, and subsequently it was this English boy who wrote of the Great Trek, not
an Afrikaner poet.

Important in studying the childhood of Francis Carey Slater is the
need to remember that his bookishness never dominated his life.
Though he read well at six, he had learned to ride before he could
read, at age four, and at eight he was riding miles from home on
business for his father. Farm work he knew, not merely from seeing,
but from doing, even plowing with oxen. There were also times
when he helped his mother with the work of the house. He was able
to cook and care for the younger children. It was thus that he received the training which caused him more than half a century
later to write that South Africans should *work more*. Then charac-
teristically he added, and *read more*.[2]

III   *School and Village Life*

When Francis was fourteen, the first great change in his life occurred. During March, 1891, he moved to Lovedale as a student
at the Mission School. A neighboring farmer, Mr. Watson, had
retired, and he and his wife were temporarily living in the house of
Dr. James Stewart (1831-1905) of the famous educational institution. The Watsons invited their young neighbor and friend to live
with them and commence his formal education. Lovedale, founded
in 1824, had expanded into a school in 1841. In 1870 the leadership
passed to Dr. Stewart, a person who became very important in the
life of Francis Carey Slater. Dr. and Mrs. Stewart and several of
their children were in the audience when in 1896 Francis delivered before the Lovedale Literary Society a lecture on "South
African Poetry." Though Dr. Stewart did not live to see the
Centenary Book of South African Verse, which his youthful friend
was already moving toward, he did, just before his death, December
21, 1905, read Slater's first book, *Footpaths Thro' the Veld*, and sent
the author a telegram.

Though lasting only slightly more than two years, Slater's work
at Lovedale was crucially important to him. This was all of the for-

mal schooling he was ever to receive. He was convinced that his teachers were superior human beings, excellent scholars, and skilled instructors. He admired and respected them, and for them he worked hard. Starting in a class containing between forty and fifty students, about one-fourth European, he ended the first term sixteenth in his group. Thereafter, he was always number one in his class. In July, 1893, a month before he was seventeen, he went to work in Alice as bookkeeper for Baker King and Co.

Both in youth and in age, Slater appears to have felt that Alice was a favored part of God's creation. Looking back upon this town in which he had spent most of his maturing years, he wrote that "Alice in those far-away days might well have recalled Goldsmith's Auburn. For it was the loveliest, laziest, sleepiest, shadiest village in the Eastern Province, and anyone entering it between one and two o'clock in the afternoon would find it almost a 'deserted village' as well. Waters, led in open furrows, from the clear sweet Tyumie river, whispered through the shade-flecked streets of the village, mingling their drowsy music with the absent-minded melodies of softly rustling leaves. The azure Amatola mountains signalled to it daily from great, calm altitudes; the sky beamed brightly upon it for about three hundred and thirty of the three hundred and sixty-five days that tell the tale of the year; and it was verily a nest of singing birds, a haunt of happy lovers, and a paradise meet for meditative poets."[3] After allowing for the intervening mists of time which always blur the details of the past, a present visitor to Alice is forced to agree with Slater that what is spoken of as progress has not been kind to this nineteenth-century village of the veld.

Signals from the Amatola Mountains, of which Slater speaks in the paragraph above, were by the inhabitants of Alice frequently answered in the form of a trip into the region. One such occasion is recorded in considerable detail and was an event of importance in the life of the young bookkeeper with his mind already focused on literature.[4] Francis had joined a group of riders having as their destination the Hogsback, twenty miles away, and usually considered the beauty spot of the Amatola range. During the day the party planned to visit with the much respected and admired Mr. Alexander Geddes, the boarding master at Lovedale, and Mrs. Geddes, who were camping in the forest near the Hogsback Inn. Included among the six riders were three of the Stewart children, two of the daughters and one of the sons. Paired off with one of the daughters, Francis found himself riding with the girl who fifteen years later was to become his wife—after she had been around the world and had lived in England. Though there is no implication that the young man was at the time deciding upon his bride, there is the suggestion that he was on the occasion impressed with feminine charm as well as with natural grandeur.

IV Banking and Sports

For five and one-half years, Francis worked in Alice. He maintained his connections with the library and the literary society, interested himself in various sports (especially cricket), continued his friendship with the Stewarts, read as much as possible, wrote poems with considerable regularity, and worked hard learning his business as a bookkeeper. In January, 1899, he left Alice for an extended vacation at home with his family, the first in many years. Near the middle of April he went to Port Elizabeth, seeking an opportunity which he felt Alice could never provide. After a discouraging search for the kind of place he wanted, he found work with the Standard Bank of South Africa, with which he was to remain until he retired from business, during his life as a banker serving at eleven branches throughout South Africa. The last years were spent as manager of the Grahamstown branch of the Standard Bank.

Naturally, after he left the farm, all phases of rural labor were denied to him. Yet physical activity continued in the form of sports. Before he departed from Alice, he played tennis, had become an enthusiastic cricketer, and a success on the track. In competition at Fort Beaufort, 1898, he won the 100- and 220-yard dashes, the 120 -yard high hurdles, and the high jump. Later he became interested in polo. Soon after he assumed his bank duties at Matatiele in 1902, which he spoke of as the horsiest town in South Africa, he purchased a horse which he undertook to train as a polo pony. As he began to learn what was required, he not only bought the proper types for himself but purchased, trained, and sold at a profit enough horses to help with the cost of his own participation in a rather expensive sport.

V Contribution to Libraries of South Africa

Few things which Francis Carey Slater did revealed more about him than the work he performed for South African libraries. After he left Alice and entered the Standard Bank in Port Elizabeth, his first assignment was for only five months, and this in a strange city. His second was also brief—in a city which was new to him and where at best it would require time for a young man to make himself known. His third assignment gave him his chance, and he was completely successful. When he was made secretary-treasurer of the town library of Matatiele, he found the premises very dirty and everything in a state of utter confusion. After seeing to a thorough cleaning of both books and premises, he returned the books to order and instituted a system for use of the volumes available. Next he turned to the economic aspects of the library. When subscriptions were all collected, there was money for additional books. Thus, the new officer immediately made a list of standard works not owned and recent books which should be acquired.

Word of the efficiency and industry with which the young banker had handled the Matatiele library must have spread because now as he moved from one bank branch to another, each town to which he went called upon him to help with the local library. When he accepted his final assignment, as manager of the bank in Grahamstown, he found waiting for him, now in a large and important town, membership on the Rhodes College Council and the usual place as treasurer of the public library. Before he retired, he had become chairman of the Rhodes College Council Finance Committee and chairman of the public library. Obviously, South African libraries owe much to Francis-Carey Slater.

VI   *Early Acquaintance with the Arts*

Though he was not introduced to the performing arts at the professional level as early as to great books, he did get a reasonably early start. In 1887, even before his teens, he and his brother Wilmot had attended the Queen's Jubilee Exhibition in Grahamstown, where the music had impressed him more than anything else. In June, 1897, at the Diamond Jubilee, he had seen his first really good professional theater. He attended productions of *The Merchant of Venice, Othello,* and *The Bells,* staged by an understudy of Henry Irving. Eight years later Francis was to see Irving himself and to know that his South African introduction was by a competent performer. Francis had heard his first opera when he went to work for the Standard Bank in Port Elizabeth in 1899. Here he saw a

London company in performances of *Faust* and *Il Trovatore*. Six years later in London he was to hear Melba in *Faust* and Melba and Caruso in *La Bohème*, at Covent Garden.

One of the disappointments of Francis Carey Slater's life was that he was unable to go to Oxford. Dr. Stewart had suggested to the elder Slater that the boy be prepared for the university, but at the time the family resources would not support such a move. It is easy to appreciate how a good student must have felt about foregoing a chance to attend Oxford, but it may be that some fate was saving him for a very special work that he was to do for South Africa. An English university education might have adulterated his South African consciousness. As things arranged themselves, he approached his writing and editing with a pure though naïve state of mind.

CHAPTER 2

Tracing Footpaths Through
the Veld, 1905

W HEN in his middle seventies Francis Carey Slater started
to write an autobiography, his first five words were "I am a
South African."[1] For all who know his writing, his attitudes, and
his actions, these words are absolute in their accuracy. At a crucial
time in the development of the literature of his country, Slater performed the task of offering that which was very much of South
Africa. Where his work is to be placed as literature is not the initial
concern here. The fact of importance is that it was necessary for
literary efforts to become South African before any work would
transcend locality and be identified as literature from a universal
point of view.

   Though in 1905 the youthful Slater was frequently employing
subjects and a style which had been exhausted, he at times was using
a substance which could be made into a literature belonging to his
country. In several ways the initial offering of his first volume projected what was to become the work of his life. The opening lines of
"Footpaths Thro' the Veld" anticipate quite directly *The Karroo*
(1924), *Drought* (1929), and parts of *The Trek* (1938). Here was
introduced the sun-seared South African soil, identified as "Monster," an unusual word in the verse of the period and place. It was
not his literary training but his experience with the simple actuali-
ties of the physical world around him which elicited such a word.
Slater knew that in this land a time of drought could destroy both
man and animal. The footpaths through the veld, then, are not
byways for romantic excursions but a structural device for directing
the reader to the human elements present in the scene. There are,
of course, the "Dark Folk," who become the object of considerable
attention in this first book, in subsequent books, and finally after
thirty years were to have assigned to them a volume by name. Sec-

ond, there are the European settlers, the farmers, who developed the land and made it fruitful. His tribute to them was written into his autobiography called *Settlers' Heritage* and in lines titled "The Settlers' Churchyard." The third path through the veld leads to the missionaries. It would be irrelevant at this time to survey the place taken by the missionaries and mission schools and hospitals in the development of South Africa. What is needed is an understanding that Slater's attitude is not only his but that of the time and place. Thus his footpaths lead to fundamental characteristics of his country.

Even in this 1905 volume, the author is beginning to work with the Xhosa materials. First there is a herd boy's song. Then he relates a story of the native practice of Ukutwala (the carrying away of a bride), in this instance without the parents' knowledge or the girl's consent. Next he presents a wife working in a maize field and gives the song she sings to the child strapped upon her back. He also writes of the homeward journey of men who have been laboring in the mines. Finally, he offers a Xhosa lullaby. Of the five, four were retained in *Dark Folk*, thirty years later, and also in *Collected Poems*, fifty-two years after this first volume.

Soon after his fourteenth birthday, Slater completed "The Palace of Poesy." The composition, which had been motivated by a dream, was looked upon by the young author as his masterpiece. It was included in his first book and two years later (with six other early pieces) was presented by E. H. Crouch in *A Treasury of South African Poetry and Verse*. Today as one reads through "The Palace of Poesy" searching for anything which will indicate later development, he receives one directional hint within an otherwise almost useless mass. The young writer decides that the Palace of Poesy is not to be reached by sailing the Sea of Knowledge or climbing the Mountain of Thought but rather that the Palace was built upon

> . . . the plains of Life, where live and die

> "Mankind, in joy and sorrow, smiles and tears,
>   In aspirations great, in longings vain,
> In strife and sin, in gloomy doubts and fears. . . ."

> "Therefore be not cast down nor yet afraid,
>   For if in singing thou dost ever strive
> To comfort fellow-travellers thro' life's glade,

"To cheer them on, their failing hopes revive
  With the glad tinkle of thy simple lays,
Thine efforts shall be blest; thy songs survive

"In some fond hearts . . .

". . . only songs born of the authentic thrill
  Of soul-pulsations truly reach the soul
Of man, and there strike answering chords."[2]

The young writer having identified his sources of raw material immediately proceeds to state what he believes to be the work of the poet as he offers his compositions to a reading, or not yet reading, world. His conclusion is that only the "authentic" will have an effect upon the receiving souls of those who read or hear. These lines, the work of a fourteen-year-old, with every indication that they were deeply felt, give one reason to believe that he will again be heard from on this subject.

Published when he was twenty-nine, Slater's first volume represented a focusing of twenty years of writing—from childhood to maturity. The Xhosa poems seem to have been motivated rather suddenly by a return to the scene of his youthful environment at the time of his father's death, 1902. "Footpaths Thro' the Veld," "Lindani," and a number of shorter pieces were written at Matatiele between 1902 and 1905. To this later work he added twenty compositions from his teens. Of the whole, Slater in his seventies was to write that he had long since come to understand the lack of strength in this first collection. He noted that "Seven only of the original forty-two have been retained (four in revised form and three rewritten). . . ."[3] While in old age the author was able to see the weakness of his writing, he was in the early years only very slowly feeling his way toward what he wished to retain. The value of the Xhosa songs and stories should have been obvious, but nothing else was easy for him.

Rightness in the use of the native materials was quickly attested by remarks from reviewers in both South Africa and England. First one title and then another was selected for praise. This variety in choice, essentially a matter of taste, suggested the desirability of adding to the five already written. Thus, through many years, the author continued to write Xhosa portraits and stories, until he finally revised and collected all that he wished to retain and published them in the *Dark Folk* volume. Connected with the use of Kaffir materials is the observation by one reviewer of this first book that when Slater concerns himself with "home things" he "writes with purpose and conviction."[4] The other areas of value were in only a faintly incipient state in 1905.

Certainly it is not without significance that the initial lines in the first volume written by Francis Carey Slater speak of the veld, pronounced "felt." In South Africa *veld* was the name given by the Dutch to any open country with grass and bushes but few trees, trees being very scarce in this part of the world. To the noun, South Africans attach various modifiers. Thus they say "high veld," "low veld," "bush veld"—to designate various extremes. Slater's own veld was in many ways a combination of these characteristics, between high, low, and bush. High or low or bush, one quality which was always present was the burning South African sun. Though from a literary point of view he does not yet do much with the possibilities of his setting, Slater is aware of its characteristics from the beginning, as the following passage will establish. These are the initial lines of his first book.

> Monster—tearless and voiceless, in agonised,
>   parch'd palpitation—
>   Throbbing in poignance of·pain 'neath the
>   fierce lash of the Sun!
> Respite is proffer'd thee only when Night—who
>   comforts the vanquished
>   Pale from the comflict of Day—giveth surcease
>   to thy woe,
> Wipes thy wounds with her tresses tirèd with
>   stars and with planets,
>   Sheds on thy shuddering limbs tears of
>   compassionate dew.
> Ocean of red-brown billows arrested and stayed
>   in their motion,
>   Stayed by a mandate Divine, stilled by a
>   whisper of God!
> Wilds of august isolation, majestical spaces of Silence,
>   Regions of vastness undream'd, home of the deso-
>   late Winds:
> List to the fugitive numbers, which fall from a
>   nameless minstrel,
>   Who in thy grandeur austere finds argument
>   meet for a song,

> Who in thy bare, brown deserts finds beauty
> which calms and which gladdens—
> More than the sensuous tints and splendours
> of Spring-lov'd lands![5]

Here in the first stanza of "Footpaths Thro' the Veld" is displayed an example of an author working with literary methods no longer of use in a period now struggling to find new forms. The years which created the style of "List to the fugitive numbers" did not offer methods capable of handling "Monster—tearless and voiceless, agonized, parched . . . fierce lash of the Sun. . . . isolation, . . . bare, brown deserts. . . ." It should be remarked at once that this type of diction is rare during the first nineteen years of Slater's publishing life. Only the veld seemed capable of suppressing even for a moment the author's romantic nineteenth-century "poetic" diction.

Some reviewers were impressed with Slater's lines written at the time of the death of Cecil Rhodes. One spoke of "In the Matoppos" as among the best of the poems on this subject. It was said to be "simple, grand, and deep" and to have "finality."[6] The author has remarked that "This lyric represents my first, as well as my final conception of Rhodes better perhaps than anything I may record in prose."[7] The lines do indeed have about them a directness and simplicity which was not usual in the 1905 volume. Three stanzas will give a suggestion of what Slater could write under such conditions.

> Like to the Hebrew seer of old,
>   Who, within sight
> Of promised Canaan, passed away
>   On Nebo's height—
>
> So he: he only saw the dawn
>   Of promised day
> Break o'er the hills of his lov'd land:
>   He might not stay
>
> To see the splendour of that noon
>   For which he wrought
> Thro' the long, weary, waiting years
>   With anxious thought.[8]

In a revised form, the tribute to Rhodes was retained in *Collected Poems.*

Because so very little of the early material has ever been re-printed, even in a rewritten form, a complete study of Francis Carey Slater must give samples of what he was writing in these formative years. Here are two illustrations.

> There's a cloud on the mountain—
>   Far away, far away—
> A dove with wavy winglets golden-grey;
>   See, it sways in sweet unrest
>   On yon peak with pallid crest,
> Gleaming in the light of dying day—
> Living in the light of dying day!
>
> Now that dove-cloud has vanished
>   Into air, into air,
> And the mountain peak lies lone, and bleak,
>   and bare;
>   But that moment's fervid bliss—
>   Oh, that cloudlet's clasp and kiss—
> Blooms, a rose in Memory's garden fair,
> Blooms and blows in Memory's garden fair![9]
>
> I would I were a bard of fame,
>   A bard with laurel crown'd,
> With great acclaim my Lady's name
>   The world to sing around!
> But tho' your praise in loving lays
>   I sing till earth resound,—
> My sweet, my dear—by heaven I swear
>   This solemn vow—
> My love for you were not more true
>   Than now![10]

It is easy to imagine what a magazine editor or a publisher's reader would do if material of this kind arrived in his office today. Though no present reader is likely to select additional titles to add to the seven the author has preserved and though no reader will prefer an early to a later version, current readers should not ignore what Slater was working toward in a climate of opinion not designed to germinate artistic excellence.

CHAPTER 3

Prose Stories from the
Sunburnt South, 1908

READERS of Francis Carey Slater's *Footpaths Thro' the Veld* learned something about the author's experiences, much about his literary past, a little about his state of mind in 1904—but they found a scarcity of evidence upon which to predict the future. The stories in *The Sunburnt South* are much more useful as a revelation of the writer at the moment and in suggesting what he would become. In time of composition, the stories represent the immediate present. All were composed within a period of six months. He started work on this series of prose narratives soon after the Standard Bank moved him to Dordrecht. When they were finished, he sent them to an aunt in London. Very quickly she found a publisher. Thus the book demonstrated exactly how he was writing in 1908.

What has happened between Slater's first book and his second is indicated by the fact that the author wished to retain, even in revised or rewritten form, less than 17 percent of the first book but 100 percent of the second. All of the stories of *The Sunburnt South* were reprinted in a final collection of prose narratives. In both instances his judgment was correct.

I *South African Materials*

Though in its thematic characteristics each of the stories in *The Sunburnt South* might come from any part of the world, its particular details identify it as South African. The most complete illustration of the use of local materials may be found in the sketch called "An African Artist." In a note Slater gives the action as taking place in East London, where he had served a two-year appointment with the Standard Bank, after five months of training in Port Elizabeth. A person who resembles the author himself becomes the narrator of the story. The men in his office are a part of the setting and make some contribution to the action. The other two characters are Paul Mpamba, the office messenger, and his nephew Manzi, who has recently come to live with him. The boy, nine or ten, dies after a few months with his uncle, despite the efforts of doctors, hospital staff, and the attention of the office group.

Building his story around Manzi, Slater introduces South African material of several kinds. Because the narrator is the only man in his office able to speak one of the Bantu languages, he is the person who can converse with Manzi. From the boy he hears various native customs, which become part of the South African substance of the story. Another means of bringing local material into the narrative is through Manzi's interest in drawing pictures. The source of the boy's passion for art is revealed as an experience with Bushman cave paintings. Even Manzi's "country to city" movement makes possible the introduction of native elements. Throughout the story a reader is constantly aware of South Africa.

Whereas Manzi introduces native material in a movement from veld to city, Moses Mpondo reveals it in moving from mission school back to the veld, in "The Red Maiden." To begin with, understanding of the title depends upon local information. The "Red" refers to the fact that the girl, Maliwe, belongs to one of the great native tribes known as the "Red Blanket" people—the Xhosas. The identification comes from the Xhosa custom of staining their blankets with red ochre. In the story the native dress of Maliwe is presented in contrast to the extreme European dress of Moses. The use is not merely descriptive but is employed as a part of the plot.

Much of the story is concerned with rather special native marriage customs—and even variations on what is itself not the normal process. All of this specialized material is clear in the context of the story, and notes establish the customs as actual rather than fictional.

II *Universal Themes*

Though Slater was consciously intent upon employing South African characters and setting, he was telling universal stories. There is nothing unusual about this fact, since stories about individual human beings must of natural necessity be universal. Only the very modern world, with rather complete self-deception, assumes that it invents original plots. Slater does not appear to have known very much about Chaucer (or was not impressed by what he knew), but he was from an early age constantly aware of Shakespeare, who had borrowed his stories, not invented them. Unashamedly, this South African storyteller in his epigraphs calls attention to what he considers the timeless and placeless nature of his tales. Each story has an epigraph, the first employing Shakespeare and subsequent narratives using Wordsworth, Coleridge, Shelley, Keats, Scott. . . and ending with Shakespeare.

Despite the fact that Slater was following an outworn epigraph tradition, he was choosing his quotations with what he must have considered meticulous relevance. For his first story, "Lena of Lion Kloof," he employed Shakespeare's "star-cross'd lovers" line upon the assumption that he was writing a love story in this tradition. Having prefaced his narrative with Shakespeare's words, he closed by reminding his reader that the narrative he was concluding was in the same line as that used by his sixteenth-century master. In the final scene the first-person narrator stands looking upon the two graves of the lovers and muses,

I thought of Hero and Leander, of Paolo and Francesca, of Romeo and Juliet and other "star cross'd lovers" whose names have been traced for all time by the golden pens of poets, so that neither "marble nor the gilded monuments of princes shall out-live" the memory of their loves: verily here, in this lonely nook, lay two worthy to be named with these.

It should be understood that except at the level of "ill-fated lovers" Slater's characters have no resemblance to the fictional persons he mentions. Lena is no later Juliet. She is distinctly a young lady of nineteenth-century prose fiction rather than sixteenth-century poetic drama. Shakespeare's young women were articulate in a way which one would never associate with Lena. American-trained short-story readers will in examining Slater often recall Poe and Hawthorne—probably never Shakespeare and Marlowe. English readers, European readers, or South African readers will recall their own parallel authors from the nineteenth century.

Turning to the second story of the collection, "The Red Maiden," one encounters the often-used "maiden-in-distress" situation, a favorite of romantic or sentimental writers. Slater has avoided both —in the usual sense. The first two sections of the story offer satire with a distinctly comic tone. Here one meets only the chief masculine character. When in section three the masculine impinges upon the feminine world, the comedy is continued. Suddenly all becomes serious and even begins to approach tragedy. Though disaster is avoided, there is not a return to the comic tone until the very end, where a felicitous twist avoids too much seriousness concerning the final actions. Far more than "Lena of Lion Kloof," this story is of the country which produced it. Here Slater is coming very close to South Africa and its native peoples.

Taking the title of his third story, "Magic Casements," from Keats's famous ode, the author enters upon the only *purely* creative effort of his book. The story is related to "The Palace of Poesy," as it actively presents the early theory expressed there.

> ". . . only songs born of the authentic thrill
>   Of soul-pulsations truly reach the soul
>   Of man, and there strike answering chords."[2]

An account of the journey of the "Minstrel" develops the theme expressed in the short story. The inserted narrative is no casual allusion to an early idea but a nineteen-page section depicting the life of a poet. Again and again the reader finds himself remembering Olive Schreiner's tale of the hunter and the fall of the feather.[3] Though it is more than likely that Slater was guided by the example of Olive Schreiner before him, she was not a unique source, and the effectiveness of the story is not decreased by the fact that others before him had used the method. Actually he has handled his materials well and has traveled far beyond the territory he has surveyed in "The Palace of Poesy."

In Oom Meihaas the author presents a South African Baron Munchausen. With little doubt, he was collecting these stories rather than creating them. Here a reader sees Slater's most extensive use of folk materials, yet nothing is peculiar to South Africa. This kind of character and this type of story is found in every community in the world.

According to Slater, "The Tinktinkie" was one of the stories related to him by Manzi, the little boy in "An African Artist." The type is as old and as familiar as Aesop. The epigraph from Cock Robin is merely additional evidence of the kind of material being employed. All civilizations have portrayed the nature of man through tales of the animals and birds—here birds are the subject. Slater has not had to localize the action, for Manzi as its source has done that for him.

Few stories are older and more pervasive than those in which young lovers are being kept apart because of some difference between the two families, a difference which has a basis beyond the personal. In stories of this type the separation is based on religious concepts, tribal affiliations, social class—that is to say any of the things upon which a society is developed, whether these be right or wrong. In "The Forest Urn," Slater has started with this ancient foundation, added to it the story of the evil councilor, and created the climax from thoroughly local materials. The girl of the story, Zenani, is a daughter of the king. She loves and is loved by Mendila, "the swift of foot, the brave in battle, the gallant hunter, the sweet singer"[4]—but not of royal blood. The young lovers have been meeting in the forest, but now Mendila learns that the king has been informed of the relationship—informed by an adviser who aims at the young man's death. A faithful friend of Mendila's father and of himself has made it clear that the young man cannot return to the great kraal of the king. With the firmness of Ruth, Zenani pronounces the "Whither thou goest I will go" determination. Zenani, however, is determined also to plead in person Mendila's case before her father. In the forest Mendila waits. Upon her arrival at the king's kraal, she finds confusion and fear. Their most dangerous enemy is approaching, is in fact only a distance of one day from them. At a council meeting, the king's chief adviser proposes immediate preparation, insists upon taking the initiative, and urges that Mendila be given charge of the tribe's warriors. Instead of accepting the advice, the king abruptly (because of what he has recently been told about his daughter) decrees death to Mendila. The council is shocked and finally prevails upon the king to think of the common good rather than of personal attitudes. He accepts the advice and appoints Mendila as leader of the tribal forces—if he is to be found. Then the king goes to his daughter's bed, where she (as he assumes) feigns sleep, and announces the council's decision. Zenani rises and hurries to Mendila, who has been stung by a great serpent in the forest. As he nears death and calls to Zenani, she arrives and in seeking his voice is also stung by the serpent. They die together.

Of the evil one who had first turned the king against Mendila, the author has identified him as a serpent. The serpent is traditional, but in Africa it is more than traditional. Here one must be ever mindful of the sudden strike of the snakes who inject poison from which there is no escape. In the story the author has with skill merged many elements.

III   *The Problem of Style*

Certainly the great weakness of Francis Carey Slater's writing, especially at this time, is his adherence to an antiquated style, a style which was never good and thus when produced for itself alone becomes thoroughly bad. As he commences the orientation of his reader for the story of Lena, of Lion Kloof, he writes the following paragraph:

> The sun sank down over the distant hills, trailing golden galleons of cloud in his wake; amorous airs of evening murmured caressingly to the listening grass which replied in tremulous, reedy whispers; from the distance came the voice of the brook, wooing with silvery speech the coyly nodding trees; and, at intervals, I heard the low of full-fed kine as they trudged contentedly kraal-wards. After meditating upon the tranquil beauty of this scene, and envying those whose lives had fallen in such pleasant places, I coaxed my jaded steed into motion and made for the farmstead.[5]

Reading this today is painful; yet it is perhaps necessary to admit that Slater's readers in 1908 preferred this passage (and many others like it) as it appears than as it would be written half a century later.

Almost all of the passages of the kind quoted above appear at the beginning, the end, or within the story when the movement of the narrative is slowed for description or meditation. The requirements of action seem to erase at least some of the padding. Here is an example from the action area of the story about Lena.

> . . . The candle had flickered out, the fire was quite dead, and the room was in total darkness. I held my breath and listened.
> Someone was moving stealthily towards the corner where the axe stood. I heard the sound of a hand brushing softly along the wall, and then the steps came towards me. A cold perspiration broke out upon my brow. The old man had particularly told me to lock my door; and now, here was I all alone at the dead of night in a dark room with a mad woman: then, too, there was the axe, why had she been groping about for that? I felt numb with horror at this thought, and lay perfectly still in my chair, scarcely daring to breathe.[6]

Seemingly Slater was not yet aware of his different styles—the shifts emerging from what he was doing at the moment. When he was "setting" a story as he felt it should be done on the basis of his literary past, he wrote what is found in the first passage. When he was engaged in the actual process of presenting action, he wrote as in the second quotation. There are, of course, exceptions and mixtures; yet the examples given seem fair representations.

One hopeful development may be seen in his description of the Karroo, in the long introduction to "Magic Casements." Though he is making every effort to be literary, he is trying to find a verbal equivalent for natural details which have moved him deeply. The following is the result.

. . . The last rays of the sun disappeared, and the wine-tinted sea was transformed into an ocean of indigo-blue, whose billows began to steal silently and ruthlessly up the rose-flushed hills. Presently only the tops of the hills showed their crimson crests above this swiftly-rising flood; by-and-by these, too, were submerged. And the clouds—those ethereal schooners, wrought and fashioned and rigged from gold more precious, more magnificent than that which poured its opulent stream into the fabled treasuries of Midas—what of them? They lay now, a dull and pallid mass of hopeless, lifeless wreckage; torn and soiled sails, battered and bruised hulks—forlorn derelicts which sent no answer back again: emblems, too, of life whence all hope has departed.

Quickly the darkness gathered. The sky still held some light; its pale-blue silken curtains still clung to the memories of day. But below, amongst the stunted bush, the bees of darkness swarmed thick and fast. A great silence held the plains, for Night was taking possession of her kingdom. Silently and breathlessly she clasped the scourged and blistered earth to her compassionate bosom, and shed the dewy balm of her healing tears upon its aching wounds and scarred visage.[7]

Regardless of what the most scathingly critical reader may think of this description of night covering the Karroo, he will be forced to admit that the figurative language shows an effort to present something which actually exists and that there is a relationship between the actual and the figurative. At least here the true direction has been found.

CHAPTER 4

Lines from Mimosa Land, 1910

T HOUGH the stories of *The Sunburnt South* represent only six months in the author's writing life, *From Mimosa Land* accounts for five years of literary activity. The volume, therefore, reveals Slater's development rather than what he was composing during a brief period of time.

I *Continued Use of Xhosa Materials*

If one ignores the section called "lyrics," the other three divisions of the book show the reader much about Slater's growth. Not only has he continued the use of native materials but he has gathered the native "songs" into a group where attention can be focused upon the identity of what is being employed. Nothing else in the book is labeled in this manner. More important, however, than the labeling is the way in which the author has started developing his materials —first of all, native materials. Three of four songs from *Footpaths Thro' the Veld* are revised and retained in the new volume. The one dropped was later to be completely rewritten and used under another title. Ovbiously the author had seen the value for him of his detailed knowledge of the Xhosa civilization, and these materials were to become increasingly important as a part of his total achievement.

Most of the native songs present characters engaged in common and simple activities, at work and at play, revealing their customs and attitudes. In contrast to the songs, the narratives reveal the uncommon actions of the group. In his first book, Slater had told the story of an instance of *ukutwala*, meaning "to carry." His note explains the custom.

. . . If the father of the girl objects to a young man marrying her, the young man sometimes carries her off to his kraal. This is at times done to hasten the marriage even when the parents on both sides are agreeable to the suit. Amongst some tribes this custom is practised without the girl's consent and against her will: this is the case in *Lindani*.[1]

Lindani was deeply distressed by her situation, and she killed the man who had abducted her and then killed the one who had assisted him. Years later in *Dark Folk* (1935) Slater was to tell more briefly, more effectively, and with more point a story based on the same custom. He also employed an example of *ukutwala* in his one novel (1925).

Using Xhosa belief, which the outside world would call superstition, in *From Mimosa Land* Slater wrote the first of his stories about Hili, or Tikoloshe (early spelling). The narrative offered here in verse he completely rewrote later for another book, and he employed the belief as the basis for a short story in his last collection of brief prose fiction. Slater gives the following explanation of Hili or Tekoloshe (later spelling):

Though spoken of in the singular, Hili are regarded as plural, and, according to old Bantu traditions and superstitions, are a race of faun-like, dwarfish male creatures who dwell in deep pools and among the reeds and rushes along the banks of flowing rivers. These debased sons of Pan are said to be extremely mischievous and lascivious. They are greatly feared by women, many of whom—to this day—refuse to cross rivers at night lest Hili should catch them.[2]

The version printed in *Dark Folk* twenty-five years later than the first form was far more effectively written, but the 1910 lyric-narrative already displays all of the basic story. This fact is of considerable importance because it shows that from the beginning Slater had found his appropriate subject matter and often the particular stories.

II *Use of South African History*

Powerful support for the claim that Slater has found his appropriate stories will be observed in the first section of *From Mimosa Land*. Here, along with "Hili's Bride," a reader finds "A Veld Patriarch," the very title binding it to South Africa, and also "King's Ride" and "Woltemaade," both widely known events. This turning to actual stories, in the latter two, would seem to be a part of Slater's determination to establish the importance of his own country on the basis of its own actions—in addition to the natural world and appropriate stories which he had already employed.

Starting as a rambling monologue by a venerable farmer, "A Veld Patriarch" ends by telling of a young man who, unarmed, fought and killed a leopard that had attacked the girl he loved. He had arrived too late. The girl died, but he lived on in a private world.

From his earliest days Slater had written about current happenings, especially the death of an important person. His first book had several brief private elegies added to one on Penn-Symons and the widely noticed "Rhodes in the Matoppos." He had also given a word of tribute to the soldiers who died in the struggle between the English and Dutch of South Africa and likewise had written in praise of Dr. James Stewart and Cecil Rhodes while they were still living. This was all very natural, but he was now moving back in South African history for his subjects. The first event he selected had occurred more than a century before Slater celebrated it in verse. The author cites as his source the following passage from Theal's *History of South Africa*:

There were five Indiamen in Table Bay on the 1st of June, 1773, when a gale from the north-west set in. A little after dawn, one of them—the outward-bound ship, *Jonge Thomas*,—was driven from her anchors and cast on the beach beyond the mouth of the Salt River. It was seen that the wreck could not hold together long, but for some time nothing was done to save the crew. In the course of the morning, however, a dairyman named Wolraad Woltemaade visited the scene of the disaster. Woltemaade, who was mounted on a powerful horse, dashed into the breakers and reached the ship's side. With two men holding to the horse's tail he returned to the shore, and this feat he repeated until he had saved fourteen of the crew. In the next venture he was swept under a breaker and was drowned.[3]

Though the author is oversolicitous in his attempt to make sure the reader appreciates Woltemaade's actions, he is making a serious effort to present the actual event. After picking at the subject in the first stanza, he starts his direct presentation.

> Out in the roar of that raging water,
>   Lash'd by the tempest's unsparing scourge,
> A ship flies . . . Crash! . . . It is torn—it is spitted—
>   By rock-fangs hidden in seething surge![4]

Slater's final emphasis in the story is his speculation upon the source of Woltemaade's courage. The distinctly South African quality of the reasoning shows in his identification of the source as the "quiet farmstead," the "wind-kiss'd kopje and sun-swept plain." Thus it was the country itself which imparted to him the heroic nature that made possible his deeds. Here, perhaps quite unconsciously, Slater is showing some of the attitudes which lie at a very great depth within himself.

By the 1840's, the period of the event depicted in "King's Ride," the Great Trek of the 1830's had brought large numbers of Dutch to the area in which the story begins. During 1842 a small British force was besieged in Port Natal, now Durban, by attacking Boers. The condition of the English force was desperate, and the one hope was rescue from the sea. Appraising the situation, Richard King determined to ride to Grahamstown for aid, nearly six hundred miles, much of it through enemy country. His ride took nine days, traversing rough and trackless country cut by many rivers, filled with wild animals and snakes and much of the area inhabited by native tribes. Courage and great effort carried him through and relief was sent by sea to the forces at Port Natal. From history Slater was transferring the event to the world of literature where it might have another chance to live.

III *From Topography to History to Eternity*

Early in life Francis had lifted up his eyes to two peaks of the Amátola range, Hogsback and Gaika, and it was to be expected that in one way or another he would make them a part of what he wrote. Though he did not retain these lines of 1910 in his collected work, here is how in this early period he felt and wrote about Gaika's Kop.

> Warrior-peak that, steadfast and unwavering,
>   Dost from year to year thy vigil keep—
> Gazing deep into the gates of distance,
>   With proud eyes uncomforted by sleep.
>
> Thine attendant damozels do arm thee—
>   Dawn, with rose-hued harness barr'd with gold;
> Day brings unto thee an azure armour;
>   Night, a hauberk gemm'd with stars untold.
>
> Arm'd by these thou watchest o'er the country,
>   Peaceful now, where in the days long dead,
> Warrior-chief, they namesake, royal Gaika
>   Dusky legions into battle led:
>
> Bloodstain'd are these quiet, sloping valleys—
>   Where the red-brown grasses proudly wave,

> Heedless of the requiem they whisper
>   Over many a heathen-warrior's grave:
>
> In these woods—now wrapt in noon-day slumber—
>   In these woods—where loud the lories call,
> Where the arums glow in starry splendour,
>   'Neath the kisses of each waterfall—
>
> In these woods, of old, the war-like savage—
>   Driven from the battle's stormy tide—
> Swarm'd: for here he found a sanctuary,
>   Here a place wherein to lurk and hide.
>
> Vanished are the days of blood and warfare,
>   Assegai and gun are laid aside;
> Orange-orchards gleam, and cornfields ripen,
>   In the vales where heroes bled and died.
>
> Lo, to us, the Past is but a story—
>   Whilst to thee, it is a chart unroll'd:
> In the future—veil'd from us and hidden—
>   Dost thou see the promis'd Age of Gold?
>
> Watching on in mighty isolation,
>   While men come, and cloud-like pass away:
> Watching on in silent expectation,
>   For the coming of that greater day![5]

In trying to examine what Slater is doing here, it might help to remove the "thy . . . Thine . . . thee . . . thou" tone; also the "Dost . . . watchest . . . 'Neath . . . Lo . . . Whilst" phrasing. Returning the "e" to the "ed" suffixes may give some comfort to the modern eye, and neutralizing words such as "savage," where nothing more than "warrior" is really meant, will increase the focus of the whole. What is left, meaning the fundamental thought structure, is quite effective. Gaika's Kop, the Warrior-peak in the Amatola range, offers a successful device for merging the transitoriness of a tribal chieftain, or any *man*, with the timelessness of the natural world, here almost, though not quite, standing for the principle of the eternal. Thus it is the Warrior-peak, not the chieftain long dead, who has viewed the past, is seeing the present, and will be able to observe the future. To mortal man "the Past is but a story," but to the land itself the

past has been directly observed and "is as a chart unroll'd." One
gathers that what the author is intent upon is getting at reality,
rather than what stories say was reality. Of course Slater, as man
himself always does, has decided what the reality in this instance
happens to be. It is a fact that "Assegai and gun" have been laid
aside. Before 1910 the great tribal wars of South Africa had ended.
Likewise the battles between Settlers and the native tribes were now
only stories. Thus in the fourth stanza the author can say that the
Warrior-peak gazes across red-brown grass where once there was
bloodstained soil. The natural color of the grass of the region has
made possible a felicitous image. As long as he looks back, the author is quite successful. Even Slater lived to see the loss of hope in
the "Age of Gold" and "greater day," which he with so many others
saw at that time. Reading the list of those, in many countries, who
envisioned the future is today thoroughly embarrassing.

As a conclusion to his first volume, Slater had used "The Reclaimers." Five years later the unchanged lines were printed in
From Mimosa Land, immediately preceding "At Stewart's Grave."
The settlers reclaimed the deserts of soil, and Stewart reclaimed
human beings. It is the third stanza in "The Reclaimers" which
focuses the author's position.

> Men, the Workers, Reclaimers
> Of Man—that sanctified clod—
> And Human Deserts are quickened
> To Life, and the service of God.[6]

The generalization of these lines is made specific in the second
stanza of "At Stewart's Grave."

> O heathen-warrior of a by-gone day,
> Who o'er this sun-swept land once heldest sway,
> This lonely hill perpetuates thy name:
> But newer, more enduring fame
> Has come to thee—
> O Sandilli!
> For lo, thy mountain peak is crown'd—
> As holy ground!
> As the last resting-place—
> Of the Reclaimer of thy race![7]

Young Francis had first known Dr. Stewart upon his medical visits to the Slater farm, though as principal of Lovedale he had no regular practice. Men such as Dr. Stewart not only healed the body and taught the mind but also saved the soul. Francis was enrolled at the mission school for only two years, but he remained in the town of Alice for six more and continued the close association with Dr. Stewart, who supported his general interest in literature and specific interest in writing poetry. Finally, and perhaps most significant of all, Dr. Stewart represented to him human greatness not only locally but the kind of achievement which was sufficient to make an impression at the world level. Here, the boy believed, was a man who had changed the history of life on this earth.

When Francis Carey Slater wrote the lines in memory of Dr. Stewart, he was literally making a visit to the grave, in October, 1906. Here upon elevated ground in the Amatola Mountains, he could look out upon all that he had been for the first twenty-three years of his life. The words which he wrote that morning were very much out of himself and were of South Africa for the time and in that place. At this point it would be idle to subject what he wrote to a critical analysis as a literary work. What is important is that the thing he is trying to say is beginning to burn away his misconceptions concerning the nature of poetry. The future would produce struggle and even reversions, but *From Mimosa Land* offered a number of examples of development in the direction which would lead to a South African literature.

In more ways than one, with the publication of *From Mimosa Land* Slater was bringing to a close one phase of his life. Fourteen years on the farm, two at Lovedale, and six in the town of Alice had filled his mind with images and ideas which would never cease to be a part of him. When he had left Alice in April, 1899, the Standard Bank of South Africa started him after five months at Port Elizabeth to work in East London, thence to Matatiele in East Griqualand, to Grahamstown briefly, on to Graaff-Reinet, Naauwpoort, Dordrecht, Somerset East, Alexandria, and now Peddie. His migrations had introduced him to the land and people of a considerable area of South Africa. Only one other appointment was to separate him from the managership which would last until his retirement. The date which divides the first third of his life from the second can be identified with confidence. On September 29, 1910, he was married in East London to Leonora Nyassa, the third daughter of Mrs. Stewart and the late Dr. James Stewart of Lovedale.

Francis was now thirty-four. Though he had known Leonora Stewart since childhood, she had been educated in Scotland and had subsequently made a trip around the world. The wanderings of both were now over, and they started the task of establishing a home. The location was appropriate—Peddie. Slater had signed *From Mimosa Land* at Peddie, September 29, 1910. The intended association was clear. Their honeymoon was at the Hogsback, the highest and most beautiful of the peaks in the Amatola range, a place loved by both and with which they had had numerous associations. Returning to Peddie, the couple started life in a house which Mrs. Slater called The Matchbox. Peddie was only forty-two miles from Alice, home for both.

CHAPTER 5

War Verse, Calls Across the Sea, *1916*

MARRIED and comfortably settled at Peddie, Slater seems to have entered upon the most idyllic period of his life. A resident of the town is said to have claimed that "If the Children of Israel had, in their journey through the Wilderness, happened upon Peddie, they would never have gone a step further."[1] As at Matatiele and Dordrecht, he gave his efforts in helping build a library. When he arrived, the books of the public library were kept in a small room of the school building. Before he left, Peddie had a new library building, constructed through his efforts joined with those of the magistrate, a Mr. Eadie. All of the evidence suggests that at the time his days were busy, pleasant, and peaceful.

For almost three years life continued in this way, and then the young banker was transferred temporarily to replace the manager at Barkly East. After a few months the temporary move became permanent, and here he remained from 1913 to the end of 1917. Barkly East was a village located upon tableland with the towering Drakensberg to the east and the New England mountains on the west. About two-thirds of the inhabitants of the district were well-to-do Afrikaner farmers. As a child, Francis had learned Afrikaans. Now he was able to use his intimate knowledge of farming and of Afrikaans. This brought him good friends and contributed to his success as a banker.

I *World War Comes*

Suddenly the calm of Western civilization was blown into very small pieces. German soldiers were moving, and soon their action had created opposition around the world. Thousands of miles from Europe, in a remote village of South Africa, a bank manager addressed an assembled group with such fervor that four members of his own small staff marched up to "sign on." Despite the fact that Slater was to say that his volume depicting this era was probably the "slight [est] . . . in worth of all [his] books,"[2] it shows quite accurately the feelings and ideas of the times.

Remembering Drake and the Armada, Slater in the first sonnet of his volume proclaims that

> . . . All things free
> Are with us: winds will aid us, and the sea
> Shall rise in wrath to guard our liberty![3]

While expecting Francis Carey Slater to give special attention to liberty, first in relation to England, a reader is pleased to find that Belgium and France receive their due also. The sonnet on France is a part of the development of the idea of freedom with which the author is very much concerned in his book.

> Best of the brave and first-born of the free!
>   Because a monstrous, cankerous worm lies curl'd
>   About the vital rootage of the world,
> Sapping therefrom the ichor, liberty,
> That nourishes that immemorial tree—
>   For this, her ancient banners are unfurl'd,
>   And steadfastly her knightly hosts are hurl'd,
> Against a foe divorced from chivalry.[4]

As one reads these lines, he should remember that everything in this book was merely a written expression of the period. Much of the material had appeared in various newspapers across South Africa, and any profits from the book itself went to The Governor-General's Fund, not to the author.

In the third sonnet of his sequence, the author addresses himself "To the Enemy" in lines which he titled "Freedom: Our Heritage." Calling upon Shakespeare, Milton, Cromwell, Nelson, Wellington, and Pitt, the author claims that

> . . . their souls are with us still,
> Whom to enslave ye strive,—sooner shall ye
> Fetter the winds and chain the unsleeping sea![5]

Though as he gazed over the sea it was England that he saw, he was at home a complete South African. His little book was dedicated to an Afrikaner, General Louis Botha, first prime minister of the Union. Within the text of the book there is a sonnet to General Botha, "Upon His Return From His South-West African Campaign.'' This part of Africa had been under German rule, and Botha had been sent with South African forces in that direction, while General Smuts operated in the territory ruled by Germans in the east. Slater ended his sonnet sequence with ''To the Springboks,'' to all South Africans, using as his title the emblem of his country, the beautiful little leaping buck of the veld.

> Whether from farm or dorp or town ye be,
>   Memories of our bright land will stir you on
> To brighter deeds, and joy of victory
>   Will tingle thro' you like our southern sun.
> *Intliziyo zeto ziyani landelá—*
>   *'Ngonyama zamatafa, niya kupumelela!*
>
> *''Our hearts follow you—*
> *Lions of the Veld, you shall win through!''*[6]

Even under the stress of war, Slater slowly was finding his proper material. Here the South African sun has become his symbol of the deeds expected of the sons of the veld.

II   *War Lyrics*

Among the ten lyrics in the volume, the lines which most completely unite the fact and idea of war and the feeling of South Africa are called ''Heroes of the Veld.''

> They have sown their blood that we might reap
> Freedom and peace: O, let us keep
> Memories of them undimm'd by sleep—
>   *Undimm'd by sleep.*
>
> In summer when thro' the veld we fare,
> And earth is sweet in the evening air,
> The red grass will ripple their names to us there—
>   *Low, sweet and clear.*
>
> On winter eves when the sun dips red,
> And lone winds rustle the grasses dead,
> We shall feel them around us, our boys who bled—
>   *Our brave who bled.*
>
> While we plough and sow, or hoe, or reap,
> While we kraal our cattle, or fold our sheep,

We shall think of them sadly, our lads who sleep—
  Across the deep.

When the toils and trials of day are done,
And we gather and circle the old hearthstone,
We shall speak of them softly, our dear ones gone—
  Our great ones gone![7]

III *Peace and War*

Viewing the natural beauty of Barkly East, Slater often found
himself contrasting the struggle of blood in the outer world with
the peace which was near. This fact seems to have been impressed
upon him by his solitary walks. One sonnet, which he called "Peace
and Strife," ends with a very direct statement of this feeling.

> . . . I can scarce believe
>   That at this moment nearly half the world
> Is wrapp'd in flames of devastating war,
>   And fiery nation is on nation hurl'd
> 'Mid shrapnel shriek and ravening cannon's roar . . .
>   —Ah, God defend and bless them without cease
> Who purchase with their blood—for me—this peace![8]

Apparently the attitude led Slater to the composition of "A Song of
the Springbok Country," which he prefaced with the statement
"Written Among the New England Hills," the mountains to the
west of his village. The lines begin with dawn and end with the
coming of evening. At noon, suddenly into the peace of this scene
is obtruded the question, "How does it fare in France today?" Thus,
regardless of where he is or what he is doing, Slater's mind never
gets very far away from the war in Europe. At the same time his
thoughts never move very far away from the South Africa which he
knew—the grass of the veld, the mountains in the distance, the sun
and clouds—then the people. Slowly his environment is possessing
his written pages.
  Suddenly into the midst of war verse in which phrases and senti-
ments of the period have been reproduced over and over, come
lines that depict mental derangement moving, withdrawn from the
human into the natural world and presented in terms of animals.

> Deep in the dim woods I wander like a wild thing,
> Where the green leaves quiver, where the waters sing;

Where the glad birds carol, where the serpents creep,
Daily there I wander, nightly there I sleep.

Sometimes, monkey-like, among the boughs I bound,
Sometimes, a tortoise, I grovel on the ground;
Sometimes, an antelope, I couch among the fern;
Sometimes, a lizard, upon the rocks I burn.

Scorch'd by the sun or wither'd by the wind,
I wander among wild things, for wild things are kind;
Drench'd by the dew or smitten by the rain,
I wander in the wild woods and feel no pain.

Sometimes, suddenly, come glimmers of the days,
When I was human and walk'd in human ways;
Voices and echoes, and old unhappy dreams,
Visit my slumbers when the ghost moon gleams.[9]

Rhythm and images here, along with external evidence, return the
reader to some of the native narratives and lyrics and certain areas
of Slater's prose fiction. Even in the midst of war, he had not lost
one of the elements which would finally become an important part
of his literary reputation.

CHAPTER 6

More Verse,
Settlers and Sunbirds, *1919*

I N December, 1917, the call came for which Francis Carey Slater had been waiting. He was to be manager of the Standard Bank in Grahamstown. When he arrived, he found himself already a member of the Rhodes College Council and treasurer of the public library. He himself has admitted that his years at Grahamstown were the busiest of a well-filled life. Obviously he was trying to live two lives. For a while, however, literature had to allow business to have all of his time. This must have been especially true during 1918 while he was in the process of taking over the bank and becoming a part of the life of the community. Unfortunately, from one point of view, he had brought with him a reputation in several areas. The bank, of course, required its part of his time; the community seems to have demanded rather firmly its part of his time; the one thing that could neither require nor demand was his writing. Yet his situation called for another volume soon. Thus, during his second year at Grahamstown, he released his fifth book, *Settlers and Sunbirds*. Later he wrote of this volume, "I wish it had never been published."[1] His wish was not quite just. This is the slightest of his books, but it is not without its value to a student of his work.

Almost a third of the material is either merely reprinted or revised. What is left is the smallest collection of new pieces he had ever offered his readers; yet some of the new work is instructive. Published from Grahamstown, called the City of Saints and Settlers, the title of the volume directs attention to settlers, meaning the 1820 Settlers. The dedication is to the author's great-grandfather Thomas Slater, one of the original 1820 Settlers. "A Settler's Portrait," with which he concludes the book, refers to his great-grandfather. None of this is much more than reminiscence and a structural device, but in a later volume it is to become more, all being focused in "The Settlers' Churchyard."

In "Van Riebeeck's Rose" the author goes back to the beginnings of the history of South Africa for his material. Johan Van Riebeeck, in the name of the Dutch East India Company, had, in 1652, established a settlement at the Cape of Good Hope. For ten years he was commander of the settlement. Slater's lines celebrate the importance of an event which prompted Van Riebeeck to enter in his journal, "To-day the first Dutch rose bloomed in my garden at the Cape." Here from this early day was an interest in that which man could neither eat, drink, wear, or sell. The rose transcended the practical, and this was a value for which Slater had made and was making still a sacrificial effort.

Much of the volume is concerned with the identification of characteristic things in the South African scene—sunbirds, butterflies, cape canaries, mimosa trees. Naturally this is more significant cumulatively than individually, yet some of the individual efforts appear to have pleased the author.

Evidently Slater was satisfied with what he had achieved in "To Butterflies" because he reprinted it later.

> O lovely, lustrous things—
> Whose iris-tinted wings
>   Fit sunshades are and gay
>   For languid flowers—
> I've watched you perch or prance
> Flit, flutter, dive, and dance,
>   I've watched you at your play
>   For hours and hours!
>
> Thoughtless—a whim to please—
> At times I sought to seize
>   Your loveliness, but you
>   Oft baulked desire:
> And if by chance I caught
> You, I was sadly taught
>   That your bright tints die too
>   When you expire!
>
> O butterflies of song—
> That I, with yearnings strong,
>   Have striven long to clasp
>   My gloom to banish—
> Your fairest say me nay,
> With flaunting wings and gay

> They still elude my grasp—
> Still vanish!
>
> Your fairest fly, and such
> As I, with eager clutch,
>   Have snatched,—poor bruisèd things
>   Are all my capture:
> Frail things of broken back—
> Dead things that lustre lack—
>   Reft of the radiant wings
>   I chased with rapture![2]

From his very early years Slater had pursued an ideal of literary creation but had never been able to capture the ideal. His long interest in what these lines say is obvious.

At times in this volume a concentration of South African materials may be seen in a brief passage.

> The red-brown grass is motionless,
> But 'neath the sudden wind's caress
> It ripples into smilingness.
> Now from tall rocks the conies peep,
> And, see, a lizard lies asleep
> Upon that sun-baked stone, while high
> Circling through the quiet sky
> An eagle sweeps. . . .[3]

Here is the red-brown grass which had been used effectively in "Gaika's Kop"; the conies among the tall rocks found in one of the bitterest passages of *Drought*; the lizard upon the sun-baked stone, which anticipates William Plomer's scorpion on a stone; and finally the eagle of "The Dead Eagle," which Roy Campbell praised. Slowly Francis Carey Slater moved toward his destination and his destiny. The years of domination by the literary voices of the lands beyond the sea would finally end. Henceforth what he wrote needed to be his own.

CHAPTER 7

An Attempted New Start, "The Karroo," 1924

M OVING to Grahamstown was one of the crucial events of Francis Carey Slater's life. Then into his forties, he had reached the top of that phase of the business world to which he had given his attention. At last he could settle in one place for more than a few months, or at best a few years. The place, too, was congenial to him. The goings and comings of the family during his youth had centered upon Grahamstown, making it a point of reference and for him a symbol of the English contribution to the development of South Africa. Thus he came to Grahamstown filled with pleasant memories and an approving attitude. He entered upon his life as an accepted part of the business and academic community, having an established position as an author and a good reputation for the work he had accomplished for the libraries of South Africa.

I Changing Literary Attitudes

Looking back upon this period, Slater says, suddenly it came upon him "that, for years past, I had been merely playing at poetry instead of sweating at it."[1] The revelation came while working on "The Karroo." What changed his concept of literature at this time is not identifiable with absolute certainty, but several reasonable suggestions are possible. From youth he had been emotionally stirred by poems and stories which made him observe what was around him. He began early to reverse the process. When he was emotionally stirred by a scene, character, or event, he turned this reaction into verse. Because there was little competition, what he achieved could be admired within its environment, and outside it was accepted as informative. After he settled in Grahamstown and adjusted himself to his work, he must have realized several things.

No longer would he after a brief period have a new local audience. Here he would remain until retirement. It was his writing, now, that must move, develop, advance.

Before this period of his life, much conscious attention had to be given to the bank because promotion was constantly before him. Having reached the final promotion he expected, his mind focused on his real aim in life: literary achievement. It was not hard to see what he had undertaken at fourteen, which is about the time he had commenced serious writing, would not be acceptable at forty, even to the author himself. Heretofore there was little reason to notice what he was doing. Present conditions now caused him to observe his writing rather carefully. Close accounting must have forced him to admit to himself that a new approach was necessary.

Though at this time Slater understood the need for something more than he had been putting into his writing, he still did not know what was required. Much in "The Karroo" shows him merely working harder at all he had been doing. It had been his practice to use elegiacs for his most serious poems, and here again he is found employing elegiacs. In his prefatory note he admits that prosodists generally assume the form unsuitable for the English language. He uses the form, however, and explains that he has employed elegiacs because he believes that this form will give the reader a feeling of space and of monotony. Both he considers a part of his theme. That meter can create a sense of space would seem merely fanciful. If the lines give a feeling of space, this reaction is more likely the result of statements which suggest space. For example, when a reader encounters "far-stretching away to the skyline," there is certainly no doubt that he gazes out upon space. Soon he begins to receive phrases such as "League upon league" (twice), "plains . . . melt into seas," "rolling away to the sunset," "through the limitless plain" (twice), "the might of its vastness," "vastness that endless whispers—/ Hints of an infinite Vastness. . . ."[2] Against this kind of battering it would be difficult to avoid an impression of space.

Whether a monotonous movement can create in the reader an acceptance of monotony as a part of the object being presented is certainly another type of proposition. Since the actual monotony of the Karroo is visual, it seems unlikely that a sound pattern would support a characteristic in space. The more likely result of monotony in meter is mere objection to the dull auditory pattern. In all kindness to Slater, there seems little to be gained from a close and extensive examination of his metrical achievements in "The Karroo."

More will be learned from a rigorous investigation of his intention, diction, and organization. The evidence available suggests that Slater's reaction to the Karroo was visual. He has said that when he first looked upon the area he found it "unlovely." Continued viewing, he reports, "opened my . . . eyes to . . . her beauty."[3] This observation is supported by the fact that when he started to write he packed his lines with visual images. Here are examples covering a very limited area: "parched . . . Barren . . . Rivers . . . of grey sand; they curl . . . Twisting through cactus and scrub . . . scrub, sad-coloured and stunted, Broken by stone-crowned kopjes . . . brown earth . . . stone-casqued kopjes . . . barren . . . stone-crested kopjes, lone leagues of scrub and of sand. . . ."[4] Even the most casual glance at the diction being used here will suggest something far more important than visual images. The writer is guilty of indefensible repetition. It seems that the author has been hypnotized by the Karroo, not merely impressed by it.

When Slater reported that the composition of "The Karroo" had caused him trouble, he was certainly truthful. The difficulty seems to have been that his intention went only so far as the desire to write something about the region which could be considered a major work. Yet he appeared unable to decide how to go about his task.

At some point in his writing, he concluded that he would use history as the basis for what he wished to say. Bushmen were presented as the original inhabitants. The Voortrekkers were introduced as those who merely crossed the Karroo in order to reach their "Promised Land." To them it was a barrier, a problem in trekking, which had to be solved. Finally came the English, who conquered the Karroo. Here was certainly an approach which could be used; but in his passion for picturing the region, Slater allowed himself to use eight stanzas in getting the physical area introduced. Thus he preempted half of his length before reaching the beginning of his historical presentation. Now he accords the Bushmen two stanzas. Three stanzas are given the Voortrekkers. Only two stanzas are used for the English Settlers, one for their development of the country, and one to say they are gone—two generations now into history. One final stanza is devoted to a conclusion in which he attempts to project his subject into the realm of the spaceless and timeless.

Organizational imbalance here reveals Slater's failure to understand that he was devoting too much attention to an expression of his emotions and showing too little concern for what would move his audience. There is little reason to believe that any reader will need more than one, at most two, of the eight introductory stanzas. Once the Karroo has been *imaged*, repetition creates boredom rather than greater acceptance.

Even in his presentation of the human history which he decided to employ in creating the Karroo, he fails to develop what the material offers. History had given him three human groups for his use. In his treatment of each group, he concerns himself with "dreams" which become achievements. He writes that the great dream of the Bushmen was artistic, a dream that had its fulfillment in their paintings, which have come down through the centuries. After identifying the Bushmen as "hideous, filthy . . . Hating of all that was human," the author says,

Limned they on rock and on boulder lasting signs of their art;
Brutish were they and unclean, yet—stirred by some glimmer of beauty—
    Thirsted to capture in colour the life of a vanishing dream![5]

Then at the end of this section he writes,

But looming from cave and krantz are inscribed in colours that fade not,
    Hints from the heart of their secret—symbols and signs of their dreams![6]

For some reason, probably beyond either contemporary or more recent explanation, the Bushman (with exceptions, naturally) refused to surrender—to Bantu assegais aimed from the north and east or European guns from the south and west. As a result he was systematically exterminated. In his study of the Bushman,[7] Laurens van der Post insists that man always vilifies that which he is about to destroy. So a stereotype came into being: the Bushman was dirty, cruel, treacherous, and vindictive. He was really only an animal. This concept, of course, is inconsistent with what is known of the age, range, and quality of his art, of his music, and of his development of the dance.

Drawing from the above information, it seems reasonable to say that Slater was doing little more than reproducing the stereotype. If he had possessed a firmer concept of the nature of art, he might have recognized the inconsistency in attributing to a "brute" anything approaching true art. When, however, he could explain the existence of Bushman painting only as a thirst "to capture in colour the life of a vanishing dream . . . some glimmer of beauty," he was offering a very vague notion of the source of art. Actually he is depending upon the Romantic dream and generalization. Art results, it would seem, from a knowledge of "how" which so far has not appeared in beasts.

When Slater moves on to the Voortrekkers, he develops this section upon the basis of "vision" and devotes most of his lines to iteration and reiteration of the fact that the trekkers had been celebrated "in song, in legend, in picture, and story."[8] As he commences his presentation of the Voortrekkers, he insists that he had seen them as they crossed the desert following the cloud by day and the flame by night—borrowed from the story of the Children of Israel.

Turning to the British settlers and pioneers, Slater uses less than two stanzas to depict their achievement.

Resolute pioneers, they strove with the obstinate desert,
 Laboured and sorrowed and suffered through weary profitless years;
Oft was their toil frustrated by locusts' aërial legions,—
 Oft was their labour made void by drought and blight and disease;
Yet, unfailing in spirit, they conquered the wild with their ploughshares,
 Making the wilderness fruitful, winning their bread from the waste.
Far from the land of their fathers, they waged their beneficent warfare,
 Drinking new courage and strength fresh from the soul of the veld;
Thrill'd with the spell of its silence, awed by the might of its vastness,
 Bathed in its dawns and sunsets, calm 'neath the lash of its sun—
Friendless and lone, they found peace 'neath the southern sky's
 benediction,—
 Found, in the sunlit spaces, an abiding place and a home!

Settlers and pioneers, they strove with the obdurate desert,
 Making its barrenness bloom, winning their bread from the waste.[9]

The fourteen lines quoted above are representative. Reviewing this section, a reader finds it difficult to understand how a writer who had been publishing for almost twenty years could fail to recognize certain weaknesses here, especially after he has concluded that he must labor over his verse more than in the past. Perhaps the most noticeable characteristic is the repetition. The use of certain types of words made impossible, of course, further development at the same level. When he wrote that the pioneers encountered drought, blight, disease, and locusts, he had completed what could be said.

At the same level of abstraction, he could have added two other areas—danger from wild animals and from native tribes. At that point he would discover that everything had been said. It appears never to have occurred to him that he might consider any of these areas at a lower level of abstraction and consequently in detail which would offer variety. Thus, when he says, "winning their bread from the waste" (meaning, made their living), he could do nothing in the next stanza except write "winning their bread from the waste." This waste or desert could be only "obstinate" or "obdurate," and against its opposition the pioneers "sorrowed and suffered." Two things always impress the settlers: silence and space. Two periods of the day always appeal to them: the beginning and the end. Obviously, on the basis of the method chosen, the author has covered most of his material in one stanza.

Seemingly Slater looked upon poetry as an art that was so exalted, especially poetry which he felt should be written in elegiacs, that it could not be permitted to have more than the very slightest association with the affairs of everyday life. In the prefatory note to *The Karroo*, the author informed his reader that "The germ of the opening poem in this volume, 'The Karroo,' is to be found in a short story by the writer, published some years ago in a collection called 'The Sunburnt South.' " The story was "Magic Casements." A traveler sees the Karroo from a railway carriage and reacts to the region and meditates as he gazes. Immediately the reader begins to encounter words such as "boundless . . . mystery . . . inscrutable."[10] When he turns to the lines for which the short story was the "germ," he finds "infinite . . . mysterious . . . majestic . . . Rapture . . . boundless . . . magic . . . limitless . . . magician . . . enchantment . . . enchantment . . . magician . . . fabulous . . . vision . . . limitless . . . magical . . . enchantment . . . infinite . . . enchantment . . . magical . . . majestic . . . supernal."[11] Obviously these words are scattered, but they with many others set a tone which assumes almost complete control. Writing of this kind does not emerge from Slater's lack of experience with his materials. He knew in great detail the characteristics of the region he was presenting and the farming methods of the Eastern Cape. The weakness lies in the theory of poetry. Seemingly he felt that poetry, especially exalted poetry, must not descend to the concrete and must not be concerned with conflict. Into his short stories, novel, and several of the native songs and narratives he permits the presence of the smallest detail and develops effective conflict.

Criticism of this kind need not be written if it is of the author's best work. Under such circumstances, silence would be best. Yet the writing which followed "The Karroo" was to be the author's best. The short stories of *The Secret Veld* initiate the change. Next the publication of *Drought*, at a time when he was not allowed to identify himself as the author, revealed a truly new and different Slater. After the composition of *Drought*, he made his final selection of the native pieces, and then turned to write *The Trek*. He learned slowly and very late, but what he learned saved him from oblivion.

II *Additional Material*

Among the short pieces added to the title composition of this volume is a tribute to the author's Amatola Hills.

> In childhood's days
> Oft to you I turned my gaze;
> Oft in youth I climbed your slopes,
> Spurred by eager dreams and hopes;
> When I roamed across the sea,
> Memory gave you back to me;
> Now, I worship from afar,
> Your beauty beacons like a star
> That guides the sea-worn mariner—
> With its pure and steadfast beams
> To the haven of his dreams.[12]

Though these lines will fade into any Romantic anthology, one word is of some interest—"beacons," at which one looks twice to make sure he has noted correctly the spelling, then nods with approval.

Readers will be fascinated by the number of influences which seem to be present in "The Dark House," the grave, toward which all are moving and from which none will react to the physical world around. Material from the seventeenth, eighteenth, and nineteenth centuries could be cited. The use of "evermore" as the last word of each stanza will confirm many in the belief that Edgar Allan Poe has been an influence. Yet Poe may well have been moved by Shelley toward the selection of his "nevermore" refrain for "The Raven." Actually there is probably no specific influence here, merely lines in a long and frequently used tradition. Another Romantic offering appears in the one addition he makes to the collection of native life, "Manzi," probably related to the character in one of his short stories.

Thus, despite his honest attempt to make a new start, Slater is still very firmly held by much that was stored in his mind from his early reading. The advance being made is perhaps from earlier conscious use to present subconscious. Important development still lies in the future.

CHAPTER 8

Novelist for a Special Purpose, 1925

WHEN Slater started to write *The Shining River*, he had already published six books. Appointment to the bank managership in Grahamstown should have brought deep satisfaction, and the place he held made his economic position secure. Though he seems to have been quite honest in giving his time and attention to banking affairs, he appears to have put aside literature only during banking hours. In his schedule he reserved Sunday mornings for writing verse. This comes as no surprise, but why into his crowded schedule should he suddenly start using his nights to compose a novel? Rather certainly the answer is that he believed he was carrying within him something which he felt must not be lost, and he chose the novel as the form in which to preserve this something. It is likely that he felt the novel would attract more readers than any other literary form. The important reason, however, is probably the simple fact that the novel would allow him more range than any other form: that it would permit the inclusion of a greater quantity of what he wished to save. So he set about writing a novel.

Considering *The Shining River* only as a novel would mean ignoring much of what Slater must have intended. To begin with, his South African setting is not merely accurate, it is actual. The rivers, mountains, and towns are all "on the map." What is more, he gave everything its proper name. No fiction stares at the reader from any point in the setting. The author reproduces, and thus preserves, the physical environment in which he grew up. Here is the Keiskama, the river beside which Slater lived as a boy; here are the Amatola Mountains, to which he regularly lifted up his eyes; here, too, are Alice and Grahamstown, never far from his thoughts all of his years. Not only has Slater used the setting of his own life but he has made the time of the novel the period of his direct contact with the area. Early in the book he indicates that the story begins during the 1870's, the decade of his own birth. Thus a reader finds himself becoming acquainted with people who lived in a particular place during a specific period of history. Three groups are represented: English, Dutch, and Xhosa. Slater even makes an effort to reproduce their speech, manners, everything about them. Often this is done in considerable detail. For instance, a careful reading of this book would offer one material for a modest essay on food of the Eastern Cape.

In addition to employing the novel to record in a very direct way memories of the land and people of the Eastern Cape during the last quarter of the nineteenth century, the author has preserved many of the activities and customs of the period. During the course of the action of the novel, and a very important part of the plot, the reader is introduced to the business of transporting supplies to the diamond fields at Kimberley by ox-drawn wagons. The particular caravan to which the reader is introduced carries meal, for even men digging for diamonds must eat. Before the end of the book, wagons are being driven out of business by the developing railroads. Also, while involved with a very significant phase of the action, the reader attends a picnic beside the Keiskama and a country dinner dance. Earlier there had been a dance at a wayside inn, likewise made a part of the plot.

Emphasis is given to the identifying characteristics of the people through the letters written back to Cape Town by a young lady who has come as tutor into one of the homes of the area. The young teacher is quick to notice differences and record them in her letters. It is Rhona Brookleigh who describes in detail the trailing of native sheep thieves to the edge of the Keiskama, the borderline between the English-Dutch territory and Kaffir land, where custom demanded that the trail be taken up only by order of the native headman of the territory into which the trail led. Rhona also relates an instance of the Xhosa custom of "carrying off" a girl, frequently planned with the knowledge or approval of the parents, by a man who wanted to marry the young woman. In the example presented, the girl (a servant much admired by the children being tutored by Rhona) runs away from her captors, returns home, and evades marrying the man who was her father's choice rather than her own.

Some of the customs which Slater preserves in his novel had been more briefly presented in verse. An example is his account of an *abakweta* dance, the final phase of the initiation of Xhosa youths into manhood. In verse he had used four nine-line stanzas. Now in a prose fiction situation he employs sixty-eight lines. The

novel has permitted space enough to record a detailed account of
the dress, action, and meaning of these important rites. He also
introduces the scene from which "Clay Cattle," in *Dark Folk*,
developed.

Frequently Slater develops his setting in exact detail. He is
always aware of topography and seldom misses a chance to remark
upon trees, grass, or any growing or living thing. At the very beginning of the novel he describes minutely bird life beside the
Keiskama. Nor does he neglect the snakes in this land of the sudden
sting.[1] Quickly a reader meets the speckled cobra, ringed adder,
black ringhal, and greem boomslang. In the forests he hears or sees
the crested lory, sky crane, brown hammer-head, wagtail, sunbird,
Cape canary, and South African lark along with the great cats and
other animals.

Before finishing *The Shining River* few readers are likely to doubt
that Francis Carey Slater felt that he was writing what at one point
he calls "this history" of the environment which had given him his
being. Yet reaction is not always worthy of the author's intent and
achievement. Within South Africa readers can consider everything
as past and therefore safely dead. Often in the outside world readers
will consider everything as *quaint*—thus without significant reality.
Often those who consider themselves the superior judges offer the
most inept reactions. One American reviewer announced that the
novel offered an "accurate picturing of mining and farming conditions" in South Africa.[2] How relevant this is can be determined
by observing that though twelve years of the life of the chief character are spent in Kimberley, Slater has summarized the whole
period in five pages, slipped into the narrative as a flashback after
the character concerned has returned to his home. As for farming
conditions, at no place in the novel will a reader find so much as
five consecutive lines concerned with farming, much less with
farming conditions. Absence of such material cannot be attributed
to either ignorance or indifference. Slater simply is not concerned
with what can be called "conditions." In a number of passages he
makes definite his area of interest.

Few readers will be surprised to find the author saying early in
his book that "The river has been used again and again as a symbol
of life and time by poets both ancient and modern; even the matter-
of-fact prose writer has not altogether disdained it."[3] Slater, of
course, is another writer who is about to offer still an additional

example of the river used as a symbol, but in this book the river is likewise to be constantly present as a physical fact. The great importance of the river as an actual stream is created by local conditions. "South Africa is a dry and thirsty land, its rivers are few and far between; the Keiskama, as one of the most beautiful of these, is deliberately chosen as the background for this simple story. It is hoped that the beauty of the river may illumine what is dark, that its rapid strength may quicken and support what is faint or feeble in the narrative."[4] The last sentence, drawn directly as it is from the invocation in *Paradise Lost,* is perhaps less important for what it reveals about the author's reading and his use of it than for the belief it shows in the influence which the natural world can have in the life of a human being. From a literary point of view, Slater is with little doubt here indebted to Wordsworth far more than to Milton. Yet in the novel he is probably more nearly parallel to a number of American writers, probably few of whom he has read. He is related to them by a common background, the concern with a virginal natural area. James Fenimore Cooper employed the great forests as the directing force which could create a Leatherstocking, with his honesty, truthfulness, courage, justice, and steadfastness. For Mark Twain, in *Huckleberry Finn,* evil was always absent when the characters were on the mighty Mississippi. In his novels, William Faulkner uses the one virginal area left in his part of the world, the "Big Bottom," as the place for man to be made totally accountable as an individual. Willa Cather in *Death Comes for the Archbishop* has the title character make the final decision of his life on the basis of the influence which lands untouched by human life can have upon a man. Of these writers, Willa Cather is the only one who theorizes about the existence of an extraphysical force, a quality which can direct a man's life. The extensive evidence here, however, suggests that something which men feel is present. Beside the Keiskama in South Africa, the stream which rose in his beloved Amatolas, Francis Carey Slater seems to have experienced some of the same force felt by Cooper, Twain, Faulkner, and Cather. The following is the first paragraph of the novel:

The Keiskama river has its birthplace among the Amatola mountains—frequently mentioned in the earlier pages of this history; it winds and wanders through changing scenes, and at last pours its silver tribute into the treasuries of the far-off Indian Ocean. The country through which it flows is one of the most beautiful in South Africa; it is a country of rounded hills crowned with virgin forest; of wild, wooded glens; of broken valleys waving with red-brown grass and sprinkled with golden-and-green mimosa trees. The banks of the river are lined with wild willows, whose silvery leaves vie with the brightness of the waters beneath and lighten the darkness of the encroaching forests that cluster around. In certain stages of its course the stream becomes almost inaccessible to man, for it loiters among sheer precipices, beetling crags and gigantic grey and brown boulders.[5]

Intensely aware of place, Slater is likewise aware of what has happened in the places with which he is concerned. Early in *The Shining River* he remarks,

. . . The country lying between the Amatolas and Alice is rich in historical association. It was for generations the scene of incessant warfare between the British pioneers and the Kaffir tribes. Forts were hastily raised to keep the enemy in check, and the crumbling ruins of these are still to be seen in this neighbourhood. In this vicinity, too, were perpetrated those ruthless massacres of Juansberg, Woburn and Auckland that are still spoken of by some of the oldest inhabitants. Murdered heroes and heathen warriors lie together in their last sleep beneath the waving red-brown grass of these, now peaceful, valleys. White farm-houses, yellowing wheat-fields, odorous orange orchards lie scattered about amongst these scenes of blood and ancient warfare.

The country is inhabited, for the most part, by the descendants of those who strove together in the stirring old times: hardy frontiersmen sprung from the indomitable Settlers of 1820, Dutch farmers who remained staunch to the British Crown when their disaffected brethren trekked northward, numerous natives, the relics of many a shattered tribe. Among the scenes where their fathers fought of old, they now toil together in peace and tranquility; assegai and gun have been laid aside and plough and sickle have taken their place; blood-stained battlefields have been converted into tracts of swaying mealies or rippling wheat; and the old, unhappy, far-off things are now scarcely more than vague memories and misty legends, sometimes revived before the flickering fireside of some lonely farm-house upon a winter's night.[6]

One other thing never far from Slater's thoughts is the work of the school at Lovedale.

. . . Here [Lovedale], in this lovely haunt, lived a number of simple, devout and kindly Scottish folks. These had left their cherished Motherland, away across the sea, and journeyed to this strange, far country, in order to bring light to those who sat in darkness. All honour to these earnest, self-sacrificing souls—all honour to these dauntless pioneers! The untarrying wheels of Time's chariot have sped on; change has been busy everywhere; the primitive Mission Station has become a great Missionary Institution. Its present inhabitants are perhaps more advanced upon the path of civilization and culture than were the worthy old pioneers, but who will claim for them that they are more earnest, more devout, or more kindly?[7]

Whether the reader decides that the author was skillful or clumsy in his use of a device, Slater employs a description of the river to introduce his principal characters.

Mirroring the life around it and chanting as it flows, the Keiskama is amongst the earliest and sweetest of singers. Its silver tongue carries mysterious messages from the blue hills to the far-off ocean. It is amongst the oldest of poets—who can interpret its song? who shall question its wisdom? Not man, who is as a momentary ripple upon its placid surface, or as a flake of foam that it dashes heedlessly to the rocks as it passes endlessly upon its way.[8]

A few pages beyond this passage, the reader meets Jim Foam and his mother, who are to be dashed upon the rocks by life. They will be saved by a man named Ripple, met by chance and upon the first occasion associated with Jim for little more than a moment of time. The man who pursues Jim from the diamond fields uses the name of Bubbleby, and he is assisted by Corporal Brooks. The girl who is finally to marry Jim likewise has a "water" name, Brookleigh. Tony Sweetwater is giving the dance at which Jim is arrested. Jim and Miss Brookleigh are finally brought "together" as they start home from a picnic given beside the river in honor of Mrs. Willows. In the novel there is also a Westbank and a Mudbank. As a summary, this sounds rather horrible, but dispersed through three hundred pages it may even go unnoticed.

Something which cannot go unnoticed is the symbolic value of the river. Very early the author presents the symbol, and almost a hundred and fifty pages later he shows the symbol having its influence.

The river is not only a singer; it is a giver—a healer and cleanser: man and bird and beast drink of its cool waters and are refreshed; man and bird and beast anoint themselves in its clear stream and cleanse themselves of their uncleanness. It is a bounteous giver; as free of its glittering treasure as it is with its crystal song: none ask of it in vain.[9]

He gazed down at this broad and beautiful river as it flowed along calmly between its bright borders of wild willow trees: its clear waters flashed and sparkled beneath the rays of the noon-day sun; already he could hear faint murmurs of its solemn song. How often, in those far-away days of childhood, had its singing waters lulled him to sleep: how often, when his young heart burned with anger, had its clear, silvery whispers soothed him. When life was bitter and all the world appeared drab and desolate, its beauty had comforted him. He had always looked upon it as a living thing—as an intimate and unfailing friend; next to his mother, he loved it best of all things in the world.[10]

. . . The river and his mother were beginning to exercise their old allied influence over him: had he not been separated from them, how different would the past few years of his life have been! He had left them because he loved them; that he might return to them again. He had followed the lure of glittering treasure—honestly and unselfishly at first—but presently it had enticed him into dark and devious ways.

He realized fully now that the riches, he had sought so diligently for his mother's sake, would prove an unsurmountable barrier between them: he almost wished that he had remained silent, that he had not told her the story of his struggles. By remaining silent he could have done so much for her: her life had been hard and he could have made it easy. But, as he gazed at the river and thought of his mother, he knew that he could not have hidden his secret long; the lesson taught by these two of old could not be forgotten: they had once more claimed him as their own.[11]

In these passages, Slater starts with the river as the very ancient symbol of life, a symbol of life for the simple reason that man and animal must drink. Next he identifies the river as purifier. From this point he drifts into a kind of Wordsworthian reverie. As he proceeds, however, it becomes rather clear that the influence of Jim's life is his mother, not the river. He says "The river and his mother," but Jim is unable to separate the two. Both the river and his mother are remembered from his childhood, and in his memories he has merged them. Looking at the river reminds him of his mother and her principles. As these thoughts come into his mind in the presence of the river, he attributes these characteristics to the stream, at least in part.

Despite all of his concern for the symbolism of the river and his near obsession with the moral lesson he wishes to present, Slater does not neglect the novelist's task of telling a story. Because of a father in the Huck Finn tradition, Jim Foam, age twelve, leaves home for Kimberley with the hope of making a fortune and returning to save his mother. At times his adventures upon the road would

have been approved by Tom Sawyer himself. Jim's twelve years
in the diamond fields is given as a flashback. After much hard work,
he and his partner accumulate a collection of stones worth at that
time something over a thousand pounds. The partner, who had begged Jim to take him in because Jim had owned the claim, now asks
for a division. Jim agrees. Then, under the pretense of being ill,
the partner remains in the tent, steals everything belonging to
Jim, and leaves the fields with a twenty-four-hour start. Discouraged
and finally almost desperate, Jim begins buying stones illegally.
When he has accumulated a small fortune, he evades the inspectors
and passes out of the fields. One detective, however, is convinced
that he is carrying diamonds and trails him all of the way to his
home. The detective takes up residence in the neighborhood in
order to continue his investigations.

Before Jim returns to his home, the partner who has stolen his
diamonds moves to the vicinity and using his "capital" is making
additional "capital" as a farmer and land buyer. Guessing Jim's
secret, he steals again. This time, however, the detective gets both
of his men. Before this time, the whole community has become involved in the narrative. Thus, in the full novel, the detective story
is only a small part. There is, however, something here to please a
wide variety of tastes.

In addition to the entertainment offered by the novel is its value
as a presentation of the people in an important area of South Africa
during the 1870's and 1880's. It has already been noted that Slater
had reproduced all of the externally obvious aspects of the time and
place. Yet in the development of his characters, he has made available to his readers—especially those outside of Africa—an additional dimension. The first error always made by an outsider is to
assume *oneness* in an area having one name. To begin with, this
oneness is applied to Africa as a whole. Then it is applied to South
Africa. Slater is helping destroy this misconception. More than
anything else which he wrote, his novel gives the Grahamstown-
Alice section of the country. When Miss Brookleigh of Cape Town
comes as a governess to the Willows children, she feels that she has
moved to another country. As she notes differences and adjusts to
them, the reader becomes aware of the characteristics she finds in
what will become her new home.

Subconsciously, through the names one is aware of the predomi-
nantly English origin of the people of the district. Yet as the

characters act and react, much more than a population ratio becomes evident. For example, when Pieter Pohl moves into the area,
he makes much of his English mother when he is with the English
and is careful to speak Dutch when he is with Dutch persons. Very
soon both despise him for the hollowness of his actions, but the
reader understands the honest reality of both population groups—
neither trying to be the other. Nor is there self-consciousness between the English and Bantu elements of the population—as yet.
When Jim returns to his home and meets the old cowherd, Ntutu
exclaims, "Quoku . . . when you were a small child I carried you in
these arms. . . ."[12] Now, of course, Jim is a grown man. At sight of
Jim "glad tears trickled down [the] furrowed cheeks"[13] of the old
man. That is all. Slater does not pad the scene.

Another example of the community revealing itself occurs when
the detective from Kimberley arrives, disguised as the nephew of an
English earl and the holder of an honors degree from Oxford. The
ways in which the people absorb or fail to absorb the characteristics
of the intruder tell much about them.

Though it would be impossible to claim that *The Shining River*
is a great novel, or even a very good one, a sensitive reader will
learn much from the book. Then, too, he will meet some interesting
characters. Perhaps the nearest to real creation that Slater comes is
in his development of Uncle Eb. Introduced early as the principal
actor in one of Jim's adventures on the way to Kimberley, Uncle
Eb finally dominates the movement of the whole story. As the
novel progresses, Uncle Eb grows, changes, as he is met again
and again.

Viewed in one way, Ebenezer Ripple, Uncle Eb, is the character
who in cheap fiction is always at the right place when needed and
protects the weak and the helpless. It is Uncle Eb who saves the
twelve-year-old Jim Foam from the red-haired tramp and then
watches over him on the road to the diamond fields. After twelve
years, Uncle Eb appears again (the novel having skipped the
twelve years) at the moment Jim returns to his home and his wid-
owed mother. Along with much else, secretly he pays the mortgage
on the Foam farm and avoids a loss by foreclosure. It now appears
that he has known Mrs. Foam since she was a child and has loved
her since girlhood. Of course he now comforts her from the moment
of Jim's arrest, aids Jim during the legal proceedings and the trial,
comforts Mrs. Foam while Jim is in prison, and marries her at the

end of the novel.

Another phase of Uncle Eb's character is seen in his skill with a gun, in the handling of dangerous snakes, in individual physical combat—indeed, in those things which often become the substance from which are fabricated the "tall tales" of the frontier. It is, however, in the development of this material that the author begins to show Ebenezer Ripple as a human being. For instance, not as a fabulous exploit does a reader hear about and observe Uncle Eb's ability to shoot but as a discrediting of the exploits of the neighborhood liar and teller of tall tales. The process is repeated in the "question" of the handling of snakes. A reader quickly feels the importance of context. In fact, the action which introduces Uncle Eb creates a favorable impression.

Pursued by a giant red-bearded tramp, Jim comes upon three men sitting beside outspanned wagons. Seeing that he is outnumbered, the tramp retreats behind the claim that he can defeat them one at a time. A slow-spoken, energetic little man accepts the taunt, and reduces the bully to a heap of defeated flesh in the dust of the road.

Once the fight is over, Uncle Eb transfers his attention to Jim and accepts him as a passenger on the way to the diamond fields, to which he is hauling meal. Quickly a reader begins to learn Uncle Eb's characteristics. He is efficient, kind to human beings and to animals, possessed of considerable wit, a good storyteller, and seems from the first moment to have a special feeling for Jim. There is a reason for this, though as yet the reason is not revealed.

Gradually a reader understands that Uncle Eb is the kind of person created by the country working with good material. Traveling across an undeveloped land, he knows where and how to find food and water for himself and his oxen. Good treatment of his servants and animals is wise from a business point of view, but it also is an inherent facet of his own personality. Knowing how to fight is a part of the survival requirements of his time, place, and occupation. Oral rendering of stories was one of the few available sources of entertainment under the circumstances. Men passed their stories around to others. Underlying all of this, of course, is the basic assumption that a man intends to work for his living and expects to be fair with other persons. There is in this, it should be noted, no element of naïveté. Uncle Eb is quick to detect fraud, deceit, evil of any kind.

Along with much else, one of the principal uses which Slater makes of Uncle Eb is to introduce through him a rich variety of humor into the novel. In fact, one of the surprising characteristics in Slater's prose fiction is the place he finds for humor. An avowed romantic and certainly a sentimentalist, he nevertheless accepted humor of various kinds.

Humor begins to emerge with Uncle Eb's comment upon Jim Foam's identification of himself as Jim Smith. The boy had apparently not considered the problem of selecting an assumed name. Thus, when he says "Smith," Uncle Eb observes that it is a "very on-common name."[14] This is all. He does not again refer to Jim's lie. That night, after they have made camp and eaten he becomes the teller of tales. Uncle Eb's stories always proceed on two levels. There is the surface narrative, with its exaggerations, its fantastic action; but there is also the reader's awareness that the raconteur knows what he is doing and expects the listener to get the humor on the level of "not being taken in." At times the fun can be created by the reader's seeing the listener fail to grasp the situation. A number of effects are possible. Much less range is achieved from the direct lying and the personal achievement stories of Oom Mias. The audience always laughs at Oom Mias but with Uncle Eb.

Throughout the book there are variations of the "laughing at" type of humor. When the detective from Kimberley arrives, his method of allaying suspicion is to make himself completely ridiculous—name, dress, speech, manner of approach, everything about him as an individual. In this instance, however, the perceptive reader will be made cautious by the very exaggeration employed. It seems fair to assume that the author expects this reaction. Another character at whom the reader laughs is Gilbert Flower, Gilly, sentimental, dandified, self-designated poet and lover of the "finer feelings." Yet even Gilly is not a completely flat character because his friends and associates know that he is true—even if foolish.

Despite Slater's concern for the geographical and historical accuracy of his setting and regardless of his intentness upon emphasizing the moral influence of environment (the guidance of a good mother or a true friend—essentially gathered up in the symbol of the river), the author has written a novel filled with action and humor. There is perhaps some irony in the fact that the characteristics which Slater valued most as he wrote *The Shining River*, in fact the reasons for its composition, are today likely to be ignored or scorned. Conversely, the action and humor are likely to have an appeal which the author would have considered trivial. Thus, one of the reasons for an examination of the novel is for what it reveals about the man who wrote it.

CHAPTER 9

Gathering South African Verse, 1925

WHAT was to become *The Centenary Book of South African Verse* (1925) was started in 1896 when Francis Slater delivered a lecture to the Lovedale Literary Society on "South African Poetry."[1] He had worked from A. Wilmot's *The Poetry of South Africa*, 1887, and any individual writers of whom he had knowledge. Wilmot's anthology contained most of the South African poems of Thomas Pringle and two poems by William Rodger Thomson, the first South African-born poet. Even in 1896 the very young collector considered the remaining material in Wilmot's book as of very limited value. However, before the evening at the Literary Society ended, Dr. Stewart had introduced Francis to the work of William Charles Scully, already published by the Lovedale Printing Department, 1886. In this manner the search began, the attempt to find and assemble the material which would establish a South African poetry in English. Twenty-nine years passed before Slater's first anthology was published.

Meanwhile, Edward Heath Crouch had made a collection which he called *A Treasury of South African Poetry and Verse*, 1907, an enlarged edition appearing the following year. Crouch made two other anthologies: *South African Sonnets* and *Gold Dust from South African Poetry*. Evidence of shifting taste and critical judgment is seen in the fact that of more than two hundred examples printed in *The Centenary Book*, less than a fourth had been presented in all of the Crouch anthologies combined. Yet Crouch was of value, and Slater praised him for keeping close check upon material being printed in newspapers. Many such pieces would never be gathered into a book, but not infrequently these writers offered something worthy of preservation. Thus, slowly in South Africa the process of collection and selection continued. Perhaps not in 1896 but certainly between 1910 and 1920 Slater was aware of how desirable it would be to have a collection which would celebrate the *centenary* of South African poetry in English. Though he was unable to complete his book for the anniversary, he gave it that title when it was published in 1925.

In offering his anthology to what he hoped would be a rather extensive audience, Slater undertook to explain the literary situation in South Africa during the century covered by his collection.

In order to assess, with some degree of fairness, the true value of a collection of South African verse, such as the present, readers and critics should give some thought to the adverse conditions under which such work has been produced. The European population of South Africa—scattered over a vast area—is slightly over one million and a half. Less than one-half of this number represents persons of British extraction. South Africa has been inhabited by British settlers for only one hundred and five years; and many of these years have been so overshadowed by storm and strife and tribulation that the inhabitants of that unhappy country have enjoyed very few intervals of tranquillity wherein to recollect their emotions and cultivate the civilising art of poetry. Thus, while warring with savages, quarrelling with each other, reclaiming the desert, and wresting treasure from the unwilling earth, South Africans have allowed the treasures of the mind to fust in them unused. It is scarcely surprising in the circumstances that, until recent years, education in South Africa was a luxury which only the children of the well-to-do might enjoy. . . .

As the reading public of South Africa is very small, it naturally follows that professional writers cannot be supported there. Men who give the marrow of their days to law, teaching, mining, commerce, farming and other avocations can scarcely do themselves justice when they devote the dregs of their time to literature. . . .

Another local deterrent factor, also partly due to sparse population, is the paucity of sound criticism. South Africa has no good Reviews, and her leading newspapers are so immersed in politics, commerce, and other such matters, that only occasionally can they spare space (and that is usually confined to back pages) for critical articles. The smaller papers are generally conducted by men who are not qualified to criticise literary work. But, notwithstanding the neglect with which their work has met, South Africa has enjoyed the services of several good critics of poetry. . . .

Having briefly summarised the salient difficulties under which South African poetry has been produced, it may be as well to indicate something of its accomplishment. It reflects, for instance, innumerable scenic effects hitherto unknown to English poetry. The pearl-grey and shell-pink mountains of the Cape Peninsula and its shimmering silver-trees; the desolation of the Karroo—its immense sun-washed spaces, flickering heat-waves, wonder-working mirages, gorgeous dawns and sunsets, and its vastness and silence; the grassy uplands, blue hills, and primeval forests of the Eastern Province; the gigantic turreted summits of the Drakensberg; the tropical glories of Natal; the golden and green savannahs of Rhodesia; the mine dumps of Johannesburg, and the blue mounds of Kimberley: all these are imaged in South African poetry.

South African poets have introduced much subject-matter that is new to English poetry; strange flora and fauna; the native at work and at play; farm life, camp life, life at the mission station and in the mine; drought, murrain, and locust; the ox-waggon and the waggon-whip; the British Pioneer and the Dutch Voortrekker. South African poets have also enriched the language by the adoption of many homely and expressive Afrikaans words and a few liquid and beautiful words from the Bantu languages.[2]

Making an anthology imposes certain limitations, whether the editor approves of them or not. Slater's first decisions were natural ones. He restricted himself to English because no readers outside of South Africa could handle Afrikaans or the Bantu languages. Only South African-born authors, or British-born residents of South Africa were represented. As usual, *all* long poems had to be excluded. Everything here is expected, but a reader recoils with some surprise from an alphabetically arranged collection intended to show the poetic development of a new country during its first century. Thus a reader encounters a hundred and fifty-four poems before reaching Thomas Pringle, regularly referred to as the Father of South African poetry in English. Likewise a hundred and ninety-six entries precede William Rodger Thomson, the first South African-born poet. Part of the problem with the volume can be alleviated by reference to the notes, but these are far from complete. Almost half of the authors have no date of birth given. Biblio graphical information will help place some of these in time, but then at best a reader encounters a tedious task of reconstruction. Slater was aware of the deficiency, but he felt helpless before the difficulties he encountered. Most of the feminine writers were reluctant to commit themselves to a birthday, and the editor's research time was severely limited. Twenty years later, in the *New Centenary Book*, he was to offer the needed chronological study, bringing the material up to date by both dropping and adding.

South African poetry in English started in the early nineteenth century with the arrival of a young Scot. With a background from Edinburgh University and experience as editor of *The Edinburgh*

Magazine and *The Edinburgh Star*, Thomas Pringle, just entering his thirties, came to South Africa among the 1820 Settlers. Though he returned to England in 1826 and died in 1834 at forty-five, Pringle became the first recorder in English verse of the Settlers' reactions to being in South Africa. Naturally his feelings were the result of his own background training upon which the new environment now impinged. Many years would pass before a writer who actually had known from childhood the land, the wild life, and the native peoples would give his impressions in verse. Pringle, intelligent and sensitive, named what he saw and gave his reactions. In two stanzas of "Afar in the Desert," he names the deer, buffalo, oribi, gnu, gazelle, hartebeest, koodoo, eland, elephant, river-horse, rhinoceros, wild-ass, springbok, quagga, zebra, and ostrich. Another stanza reveals Pringle's reaction to at least one area of the country itself.

> Afar in the Desert I love to ride,
> With the silent Bush-boy alone by my side:
> Away—away in the Wilderness vast,
> Where the White Man's foot hath never passed,
> And the quivered Koranna or Bechuan
> Hath rarely crossed with his roving clan:
> A region of emptiness, howling and drear,
> Which Man hath abandoned from famine and fear;
> Which the snake and the lizard inhabit alone,
> With the twilight bat from the yawning stone;
> Where grass, nor herb, nor shrub takes root,
> Save poisonous thorns that pierce the foot;
> And the bitter-melon for food and drink,
> Is the pilgrim's fare by the salt-lake's brink:
> A region of drought, where no river glides,
> Nor rippling brook with osiered sides;
> Where sedgy pool, nor bubbling fount,
> Nor tree, nor cloud, nor misty mount,
> Appears, to refresh the aching eye:
> But the barren earth and the burning sky,
> And the black horizon, round and round,
> Spread—void of living sight or sound.[3]

What Pringle started, others continued. A generation later the first South African-born poet has this to say about his native land.

> Bold mariners who sailed of old
> Through unknown seas in search of gold,
> Saw those dark rocks, those giant forms,
> And, fear-quelled, named them 'Cape of Storms!'
> O land of storms, I pine to hear
> That music which made others fear;
> I long to see thy storm-fiend scowl,
> I long to hear the fierce winds howl,
> Hot with fell fires across thy plains.[4]

The author of these lines, William Rodger Thomson, died at thirty-five, even younger than Pringle. Yet others would take his place.

When the others came, they knew their South African materials in intimate detail. Where Pringle disposed of an animal with one word, or at most several, Kingsley Fairbridge gave a whole poem to each animal which he presented. Ten six-line stanzas tell of Ingwi the Leopard. Not only did writers like Fairbridge depict the animal life of the country but also the native life. In a poem which he calls simply "Burial," Fairbridge notes that "Among the Manyika, a dead infant is buried by its Mother without a ceremony."

> YOWE, *yowe, mwanango duku!*
> I bury you here by the edge of the lands.
> Under the scrub and the weeds I bury you,
> Here in the clay where the bracken grows.
> Here on the hill the wind blows cold,
> And the creepers are wet with the driving mist.
> The grain-huts stand like ghosts in the mist,
> And the water drips from their sodden thatch.
> And the raindrops drip in the forest yonder
> When the hill-wind shakes the heavy boughs.
> Alas! I am old, and you are the last—
> Mwanango, the last of me, here on the hillside.
> The dust where you play'd by the edge of the kraal
> Is sodden with rain, and is trodden to mud.
> The hoe that I use to fashion your dwelling
> Is caked with the earth that is taking you from me.
> Where now is Dzua who ripes the *rukweza?*
> And where now are you, O *mwanango kaduku?*
> Alas! Alas! My little child!
> I bury you here by the edge of the lands.[5]

Fairbridge died in his middle thirties; yet he had broken through some of the barriers that needed to be destroyed.

Born in England in 1867, coming to Africa in 1901, Arthur Shearly Cripps spent half a century as a missionary in Mashonaland. Slater early recognized his worth, dedicated his *New Centenary Book* to him, and finally was able to visit Cripps. If man is ever permitted to judge man, a mere mortal looking at the life and work of Arthur Shearly Cripps is moved to conclude that here is reality as human beings are seldom permitted to observe it. In his thirties, Cripps settled among the Mashonas and there he remained until he died in 1952, a blind old man. Though it is impossible to reveal in a few lines much about an author who wrote extensively, his presentation of the veld has about it a quality found in none of the numerous authors who have employed this subject.

> Ragged brown carpet, vast and bare,
> Seamed with grey rocks, scathed black with flame!
> Stage-carpet, foil for all that's fair!—
> O'er thy grim stretches dance in air—
> Sun, moon and stars in dazzling wear,
> Enhancing splendours by thy shame.
>
> Poor, unloved! Take my love and praise—
> Not most because so faëry-fine—
> Heav'n peeps at poverty of thine,
> Nor because thy mute exile days
> Teach best the worth of greenwood ways,
> And meadows where deep waters shine!
>
> Nay, most for all thy weariness—
> The homeless void, the endless track,
> Noon-thirst, and wintry night's distress—
> For all tense stretchings on the rack—
> That gave me my lost manhood back![6]

Out of barrenness had come life. A mystery, yes, but one that Arthur Shearly Cripps could understand.

Interest in and admiration for Cripps was quite natural for Slater because they were of the same generation, Cripps being slightly older. What one wishes to know at this point is how the editor of this volume felt about the future. It is not clear that in 1925 Slater knew that the first century, 1820 to the 1920's, had been preparation and that around him were writers who would justify his hopes. He had, however, read and approved the early verse of Roy Campbell, who had published his first book in 1924, while Slater was putting together his anthology. The editor must have been deeply affected, however, because he varied his usual practice in the bibliographical section and remarked that Campbell's *The Flaming Terrapin* was a "work of great power and beauty."[7]

CHAPTER 10

Another Start—Free Verse, 1929

WHETHER a reader considers *Drought, A South African Parable* as poetry or not, as well written or not, as legitimate criticism or not, he is unlikely to be neutral about what he has read. Published as the work of one Jan Van Avond, the book (actually a collection of forty numbered sections, printed individually as lyrics or narratives, and with a Prelude and Epilogue) was completely different from the seven volumes by which the public already knew Francis Carey Slater. Nor did the publisher's imprint suggest the author's identity, and the dustjacket observation that the point of view was "essentially Africander" (*sic*) seems designed to mislead the reader—since it would be difficult to be more English than Slater. Though Jan Van Avond's identity was not revealed in 1929, his English attitudes were made exceedingly clear a quarter of a century later when the author, reliving the various periods of his past, recalled the motivation for *Drought*.[1] During the passing years there was no retreat from the expressed opinions (albeit under a pseudonym because of his position in the bank); but during the closing days of his life a resigned, almost fatalistic, sadness crept into what he still felt driven to say to his readers. Anyone who has known South Africa during the last decade of Slater's life will see in his sadness a typical rather than an individual manifestation among the English.

I *The Country and the Composition*

Little known through the world is South Africa's desperate need for water. Only under the best conditions is the supply adequate for anticipated needs. Always the margin of safety is slight, and any decrease in rainfall is immediately felt. In such an area drought means tragedy to all living things: man, animals, and the whole of the growing world.

From the history of his farming family and his own experience,

Francis Carey Slater had learned the effects of drought. Often he had attempted to state his reactions to the physical nature of the land in which he was born and to which he was profoundly attached. He was constantly aware of the sun and took particular delight in water, especially rain and running streams. Much of his feeling for water and lack of water, growing things and death of the vegetable world, focused in his attempts to write about the Karroo. *Drought* (1929) was his next published book of verse after *The Karroo* (1924). He took up the fact of drought again in the first section of *The Trek* (1938). It is abundantly clear that Slater was ever aware of the physical fact of drought and its effect upon all within its reach.

Though throughout his childhood and youth the future author had lived with the image of drought as a destroying force, it was in the late 1920's that he seems to have begun to equate drought and hate as destroyers. Each was the absence of something else, drought created by the absence of water and hate by the absence of love. In this relationship is found the basis for the poem. Drought is used not as a metaphor but as a parallel phenomenon. The sensory details of the poem, the basis for the reader's initial emotional reactions, come from drought in the natural world, drought with all of its physical effects. Once he has created a sense of the destructive power of natural drought, the author asks his reader to accept hate as a destroying agent of equal and like force—each being able to devastate a country.

Opening with South Africa's burning sun, the author presses harder and harder upon the reader images of blazing heat which dries and kills. Twelve sections are used to develop the drought which covers the land. The process starts when the sky appears as a "blue coiled serpent," which "turns to the earth one blazing eye."[2] Effects are noted at once.

> Bewitched by the sun's basilisk eye,
> As it blazes on through the brazen days,
> The rivers sing no more. . . .[3]

> Winds from the far Kalahari,—
> Blasts from the furnaces of the sun,—
> Stampede suddenly across the veld,
> Blazing hotter as they blow. . . .[4]

Powder is the grass, burnt powder,
Mingled now with the dust from which it sprung. . . .

Naked is the veld, scorched and naked,
Charred is its coat, once brave and green;
Naked to the sun's lash it quivers—
A victim defenceless.[5]

All that lived has died. Nothing remains except "Grey rocks, brown stones." The veld "Is the urn of beauty."[6]

Turning to narrative, the author presents the effects of physical drought upon both European and native elements of the population. Piet Bloem and his family represent the small farmers of the country. Long hours Piet labors to save his cattle, but all die. To the door of his cottage Piet nails the inscription "God has forsaken us" and with his wife and small children walks away to seek work in the nearest village. A note informs the reader that Piet Bloem's inscription was a case history—not fiction.

Next the author turns his attention to what is happening to the natives. Early in the year, the men had planted the mealies and plowed the rows. Later the women had hoed them. Both men and women had looked with hope towards the harvest, but there was to be no harvest. The merciless sun had destroyed the mealies and made hope difficult. Then the young and middle-aged men had left their homes and sought work in the deep mines. At home the women, children, and old men are forced to open the cellars in which reserve mealies are stored. The meager supply must be carefully rationed, but food is abundant compared with water—which for man and beast becomes less and less and less.

Section twenty-one offers perhaps the bitterest passage to be found among the writings of Francis Carey Slater. Here again it is fact and not fiction that becomes the basis for his observations. A note explains that "In 1927, while vast areas of South Africa were scourged by the severest drought on record, our statesmen were engaged in an acrimonious debate regarding the pattern of a new flag."[7] Upon these facts of history, the author developed the following lines, accusing the "statesmen" of an inability (or refusal) to distinguish between the fundamental and the trivial:

Women weep over their hungry children;
While our well-fed statesmen

Loll drowsily
Upon comfortable benches,—
Like sleepy dassies
That sun themselves
Amongst fissured crags,—
Drowsily they loll,
Then start up suddenly
And with animation and anger,—
With drums and tramplings of hollow oratory,—
With rage, spite and venom,—
They discuss—flags.
The children cry for bread,
And our amiable statesmen
Give them—a flag.[8]

Blindness to what is needed results, Slater claims, from "hate."
Hate blinds man as the ringhals, a snake of the cobra family, blinds
its enemy with venomed spittle that it may strike as it pleases in
its own time. Thus hate,

Lays waste our Land of Hope,
Strangling its springs of action,
Blighting its wistful buds,
Heralding sterile torpor
And desolation.[9]

In confession Slater cries,

We are fettered and bound
In the bonds of ignorance,
Meanness and Hate.[10]

We, South Africans, are children of the veld,
And many of us have inherited
Ancient enmities and corroding hates. . . .[11]

Like our tortured Land,
We have suffered tribulation:
Droughts of hate have devastated us. . . .
How long shall we walk blindly
In a land flooded with sunshine?[12]

Eventually rain descends upon the veld, and in the natural world
birth follows death. A series of lyrics celebrates the advent of water.

> Softly and quietly across the waiting mountains,
> Softly and quietly and while we slept in sorrow,
> Sure of its way even in the heart of darkness,
> Came the redeeming rain. . . .[13]

Once more a drought has ended; again the land is green. Cattle reappear on the plains and sheep on the hills. Streams become musical, and birds sing in the foliage above them. Once more nature has brought about a balance. Now the author prays that love will come to banish hate.

> O may love come, like shining rain,
> Our souls to liberate,
> To burst for us the searing chain,
> The serpent-skin of Hate. . . .[14]

These lines were composed near the end of 1928. Twenty-five years later when the author wrote his autobiography, he was still waiting for the love which would liberate. Even if Slater were here today, he would not find the love which would fall like the rain that broke a drought. It seems reasonable to say that in relation to this particular situation he died a disappointed man. The only way he could have avoided this would have been to live in many other countries as he lived in South Africa. Then he would have known that what he found in South Africa was not unique, not even special. In fact, it was and is very general, indeed universal.

II *Evaluation*

Both during the period of composition and at the end of his life, when he looked back upon his writing, Slater was concerned about the methods used for the creation of *Drought*, and he was intensely aware of its reception. Before 1928 he had used traditional forms, but now turned to free verse. Exactly a quarter of a century separated this volume and the author's first book; therefore, to him the break with traditional forms meant more than it could mean to the outside world of writers and readers. This point of view is supported by the fact that only a small percentage of the comment upon the book was in terms of its form. A sampling of press clippings which author and publisher wished to display will reveal that part of their hopes which had been realized.

Remarkable for its remorseless power. . . . A moving piece of work . . .
unusually strong and vivid. . . . A beautiful poem and terrible in its beauty.
. . . Pictorial truth and imaginative force. . . . Expertly unmerciful. . . .
Paints a real South African landscape—paints it until we feel the horror
of the parched and naked land. . . . Passages of real power and poignance.
. . . Full of extreme and legitimate imagery. . . . Strong and sincere. . . . Dry,
sparkling and tonic as the air of the Karroo. . . . Virile earnestness and vivid
imagery. . . . A truly remarkable poem. . . . It is difficult to understand why
it is called a poem. . . .[15]

Excerpts from letters written to Slater reinforce the position taken
by the press.

I think of *Drought* as the best of all poems of the Cape. (Ian D. Colvin)[16]

. . . you have given fire and strikingly original treatment to a great subject.
I welcome it as a promising sign of a new strength to be added to the body
of English poetry—the strength and reality of Colonial experience. This is
poetry in contact with actuality—and at the same time it is scrupulous art
as well as vivid stuff. (Lascelles Abercrombie)[17]

My first impression of *Drought* was that it was the work of a young man,
simply because it is frank, outspoken and high-spirited. It makes no
difference to my aesthetic response to the poem to know that it·is the work
of an older man. It only enhances my moral respect for the author, as it
is a rare thing for any man to preserve his integrity till middle-age in
a country like South Africa where so much depends on astuteness and
duplicity. (Roy Campbell)[18]

I think "Drought" is a great poem. . . . (T. J. Haarhoff)[19]

Passing of time often is said to make more accurate the critical
evaluation of a piece of writing because of increased perspective
through a sloughing away of those concerns of the moment which
create prejudiced readings. In considering *Drought* one might
suggest that even the author himself could be expected to forget
after many years the bitterness with which he received a particular
action of Parliament; however, Slater's statements in his autobiography (1954) reveal no diminution of the feeling displayed in
1929. Here a reader should not be led to believe that the original
emotion has survived the passing of twenty-five years but that
succeeding events have created similar or even identical reactions.
Thus the general attitude remains unchanged.

When an observer moves from within South Africa to the ouside world, he discovers a growing rather than a diminishing awareness of all parts of Africa. Knowledge and understanding, however, have not developed as rapidly as awareness. As a result, detached criticism is difficult, for few wish to discuss literature as literature. If the subject and point of view please, the work is praised; if they displease, the work is condemned. Literary criticism should be concerned with an evaluation of the total impingement of a piece of writing, not with the critic's approval or disapproval of the ideological implications of what he has before him. Examined as a literary composition, *Drought* has several things that deserve serious consideration.

Perhaps no reader will object to the claim that the author has handled the narrative areas with effectiveness. One section tells the story of Piet Bloem, a farmer who lives in a cottage built in a tiny crinkle of the veld. When drought descends upon the land,

> Grimly Piet toils from dawn to dark,
> Chopping branches from all trees
> That have the slightest flutter
> Of green leaves upon them;
> Slicing prickly-pear and aloes
> For his famished cattle;
> Carrying water from the bore-hole
> For those too weak to rise.
> But his labours are vain,
> The foodstuffs are exhausted;
> The bore-hole dries up:
> Huddled around the homestead
> The cattle lie—too spent to stand:
> They follow Piet with patient eyes,
> Inquiring and suffering eyes.
> Piet—the only God they know—
> Can no longer aid them
> And puzzled they die—despairing they die.[20]

The Dark People, too, are a part of this struggle for existence.

> The women rise, before the morning star,
> And hasten away to draw water
> At distant wells, now daily drying up.
> As they return dejectedly,

With cans of muddy water
Balanced upon their heads,
The few starved sheep and goats
(All that are left of the livestock)
Scenting the water
Totter after the women
Bleating dismally:
But that mud-stained water
Is more precious than pearls,
And the thirst-stricken animals
Cry for it in vain.[21]

Here there is no politics. All is human and the reaction universal. If there had been no more than these two sections used to establish the effects of physical drought, not even one reader would have been left in doubt.

In turning to the formal aspects of *Drought*, its so-called free verse, a reader encounters a problem which must be examined in more detail than was required in handling the narrative sections. To begin with, it is necessary to remember that considered strictly there is no such thing as free verse, that the two words offer a contradiction in terms. Verse patterns exist upon the principle of repetition. If *only* meter and rhyme exclusion are considered, no more than a fraction of 'the total impression to be achieved from repetition has been abandoned. Thus, in the following lines, Slater dispenses with meter and rhyme as he had always practiced them but employs numerous devices which create pattern. The resulting lyric has distinct form and more subtlety than his traditional methods frequently offered.

Long have we waited,
Watching and weary,
Gazing aloft at
The speckless sky;
Why have you lingered
Shy and reluctant,—
Why have you tarried,
Radiant rain?
Now from the ocean,
Sweeping and swaying,—
Now o'er the hilltops,
Dancing you come,—

Here may you linger,
Here may you tarry,
Bless and caress us
Bountiful rain.[22]

Another section displays stanzas being formally created by the repetition of whole lines, initial words of a line, and summaries which gather up what has just been said.

Grey rocks, brown stones—
Swarming upon abrupt hilltops,
As vultures cluster around carrion;
Beading the crinkled bodice of the veld,
As ladybirds spangle the finery of a sun-flower:
Grey rocks, brown stones,—
Soulless, lifeless, uncomely,—
Deaf to the shining utterances of the dew,
Deaf to the murky roar of impatient thunder;
Blind to the dazzling eye of the sun,
Blind to the livid lasso of the lightning;
Deaf, blind and uncomely,—
Immutable and imperturbable,—
Grey rocks, brown stones.[23]

Though the above passages offer evidence that the author was concerned with form, the more valid test of creative writing is an examination of image content, a calculation of the density of what is being presented. Below are the lines with which Slater opened *Drought*, where after the Prelude stating the subject, a reader may expect the introduction of setting, perhaps through the use of a descriptive method. Description is present, yet the lines do more than create setting:

The sky is a blue, coiled serpent,
That turns to the earth one blazing eye.
Stricken by that eyeball's torrid glare
The grass curls up and withers—
Curls, as a songololo curls
At the touch of a careless foot;
Dazed, the little veld-flowers droop,—
Droop and faint, crumble and die,
And their shadows confort the veld no more;
Shrivelled, the leaves fall from the trees,

> And the trees stand dejected and melancholy,
> Like spendthrifts who have scattered their gold,
> Or like gaunt ghosts that brood
> Over the lost substance of life.[24]

Literally, the setting presented in these lines is very simple: the sky is blue and the sun hot; the grass withers, flowers die, and trees shed their leaves. At the next level, the passage becomes figurative, the sky a "coiled serpent," the sun its "blazing eye," the grass withering "as a songololo curls." As a reader proceeds he encounters metaphor, simile, personification. These are still simple and not especially significant. At the next level, however, the section becomes much more distinctive. Usually a blue sky suggests that which is visually pleasing and good. In South Africa the blue sky is seen often, but its blueness means an absence of the frequently much-desired cloud cover, the longed-for protection against a sun which becomes malignant rather than beneficent. Thus there is justification for the "coiled serpent" metaphor. Beyond justification, there is naturalness. In South Africa one must be constantly aware of possible death from the swiftly striking snake—often from above, for some of the most dangerous nerve-poison snakes are climbers. Danger from above, then is appropriate. Now the author looks earthward to effects: the grass, flowers, and trees feel immediately the sting of developing drought. Grass withers as a songololo, a common species of millepede, curls. This is an apt simile, but the important aspect of the description is not the use of something South African. The impact of the passage derives from statement of the cause for the curling action—"at the touch of a careless foot." As with the sun, the casual agent is unconcerned, even unaware of what has happened. Next, the veld flowers droop, crumble, and die. The author observes that "their shadows comfort the veld no more." Within South Africa this will be accepted as commonplace, but to those outside of the country the implication of this complete lack of shade will come with the force of shock. Immediately the scarcity of shadow is emphasized through the loss of leaves by the few trees that the region can boast. In this condition the trees as "gaunt ghosts . . . brood" over the "lost substance of life." These last four words are true in several areas of the situation being projected. Quite simply, of course, no tree can live without leaves. Then, too, the limited trees of the country not only furnish welcome shadows but vital shade to both man and animal during needed periods of rest. From an elevation above the other growing things, the trees look down upon a scene of desolation where the "substance of life" had disappeared. There is no food and no water. Man and animal cannot continue here.

Any close examination of *Drought* will assemble evidence that Slater was presenting some of the best writing he had done up to this period. In fact, there seems little doubt that this was his best. The book, however, has weaknesses. In Parts I and II he had spoken of drought; now in Part III he writes of hate.

> Let us sing sadly of Hate:—
> Crescendo—
> The hate of the Dutch for the British;
> Diminuendo—
> The hate of the British for the Dutch;
> Crescendo
> The hate of both for the Dark People;
> Diminuendo—
> The hate of the Dark People for the White.[25]

The rigidly patterned verse here is appropriate for the subject matter, but only superhuman writing at this point will keep the readers from injecting strong personal emotions into any reaction and making it almost impossible for them to keep any attention focused upon the universal principles in the total situation. Nor do the sections which follow relieve the tension. The lines immediately succeeding introduce a series of charges against South Africa, prefaced by the line, "Some from other lands say:. . . ." The accusations are concluded with the question,

> Can we, sincerely and solemnly,
> Deny all these indictments?[26]

The charges are now made against the whole country, not merely one part.

> For we, South Africans, supremely wise
> In our own conceit,
> Parade our pitiful ignorance
> And churlish narrowness
> With incredible complacency.[27]

Across the veld, rain finally descends. Throughout the pages of Part IV water falls and brings life to the land, and the author ends the section which celebrates the end of drought with a stanza which prays for love which will end the drought of the spirit. Seemingly, however, Slater can not resist a cry to action.

> South Africa arise,
> Shake off the bonds of Hate. . . .[28]

The sincerity of the appeal need not be considered, but the literary wisdom of the manner should be firmly questioned. With little doubt, one can say that the ultimate effectiveness of a piece of work has been seriously impaired by sections which need never have been written.

If *Drought* has a weakness, it is bitter directness, not free verse.

CHAPTER 11

Retirement, Cape Town, and Travel

I *Retirement*

HAVING spent more than thirty years with the Standard Bank, Frances Carey Slater requested retirement as he approached his fifty-fourth birthday in 1930. Always he had shown a real interest in his work and had done it well, but it was obvious that he longed to settle down to a life of contemplation and devote his last years to literature. The officials of the Standard Bank, though with reasonable regrets in doing so, granted his request and announced his retirement. Long leave and the end of his banking career almost coincided; so when he and his wife left Grahamstown for a trip to England, it was their farewell to the business world and to the city of Saints and Settlers. On the night before his departure, Slater was given a public dinner attended not only by prominent citizens but by farmers from the surrounding country. The mayor presided; the guest of honor was given a handsome present; and appropriate speeches were made. As the Slaters left by train for Port Elizabeth to sail for England, a large crowd gathered at the Railway Station to cheer them on their way. In triumph Slater left the town which had been a symbol of importance to him since early childhood.

When Slater retired from the bank, an institution which had consumed most of the hours of his mature life, he looked back upon those years and made a comment which revealed much about himself. The way his mind worked, the values by which he lived, even his manners and his sense of humor may be clearly seen in the following two paragraphs:

Having now come to the end of my banking career I should like to make a few general comments. A Bank's manager's life—like a policeman's—is not always a happy one; but it is generally interesting, occasionally amusing, and sometimes difficult and exacting. He meets from day to day all sorts and conditions of people and should, of necessity, be a shrewd judge of character—suffering fools with patience and sharpers with polite suspicion. He should have a retentive memory in connection with the names, faces, idiosyncrasies and the social and financial standing of his various customers. He should be deferential but persuasive in his correspondence when defending the interests of his customers against the criticisms of his Headquarters. Under strong conviction, and at grave risk to himself, he may be constrained on very rare occasions to disobey the orders of those who sit in the Seats of the Mighty. Although I cannot recommend this course, I have adopted it more than once to the benefit of the Bank. Not the least of a Bank manager's duties is the administration of his staff. He should treat those under his command with unfailing fairness and firmness, taking a personal interest in their welfare and setting them a good example of diligence and devotion to duty. To sum up: a Bank manager should be alert, astute, energetic, sound in judgment, decisive, far-seeing, patient and polite under provocation, pleasant in manner and tidy in dress. In short, were a Bank manager all that he *should* be, he would be a wingless angel. Banks are in some respects social clubs, life-long friendships are sometimes made in them, and, occasionally less-lasting enmities are engendered. Since their invasion by women-clerks, I am told that Banks have fair claims to be called matrimonial agencies.

After all of this serious comment, Slater turned to less ponderous material and finally to a story at which his readers could laugh.

I have mentioned that a Bank manager's life is occasionally amusing: it is so, for instance, when a bewildered lady proposes to liquidate her overdraft by drawing an additional cheque and depositing it to her credit. Such odd little episodes can never—or hardly ever—occur in these sophisticated times. Whilst I was in the Bank I met few—very few—good businesswomen. My general impression was that women were unsatisfactory in business matters mainly because they were apt to sacrifice reason to sentiment. Women (I greatly admire the sex) are now far more efficient in business than they were in those far away times, but has their basic philosophy changed? I have experienced several amusing incidents in the Bank, which are hardly worth relating. But one of our managers from a remote country village told me of a rather unusual application for a loan once made to him. A young *bywoner* (person who lives on another's farm under conditions of service) had walked into the village with his prospective bride, from a farm some miles distant, in order to get married. The *predikant* (parson) refused to marry the couple because the would-be bridegroom could not pay his fees, which amounted to slightly less than a pound. The youth, having been told that the Bank lent money, thereupon applied to the local manager for a modest loan. His application was kindly but firmly refused. The disappointed applicant left the office with a poignant exclamation in Afrikaans, which may be paraphrased as follows, 'O, my time! What shall I now do? She has such gorgeous outlines!' I feel sure that I would have *given* the poor boy his prodigiously important pound![1]

Despite Slater's desire to be a writer, present from youth to old age, he was in almost every way suited to his life as a banker, and he seems to have been happier making his living in this way than in almost any other way one might imagine for him.

II *Cape Town*

Now, however, he was off to England, this time for rest and medical care. Trying to live the life of a banker and an author (and recently, editor) had exhausted his strength. Yet before his stay in England had reached its intended limit, he was notified of his mother's death and returned to South Africa for the purpose of attending to family affairs. Then, near the end of 1931 he made the important decision to leave the Eastern Province, where he and his wife had spent most of their years, and to settle in Cape Town. In Wynberg, between Main Road and Salisbury Road, he purchased a home, Manystairs, approached by private lanes, where he was to live for the next quarter of a century.

Seemingly Slater and his wife decided to move to Cape Town before making a choice as to exactly where they would live. He reports that they spent considerable time in their search and ultimately examined some fifty properties. If the investigation had continued for years and covered the earth, they could not have selected a more perfect spot, for Cape Town is one of the most unusually located cities of the world. The home chosen was eight miles from the business center and offered magnificence in every direction. To the west, three-thousand-foot granite peaks were almost close enough to touch, and in the east the mountains of the Cape interior, delicately tinted, rose in the distance. Within walking range were the University of Cape Town, beneath Devil's Peak, Wynberg Park, Kirstenbosch botanical gardens, and the Rhodes Memorial. Nearby was Zeekoe Vlei, and in Cape Town one is ever aware of either the Atlantic or the Indian Ocean. Even a bus trip into the city from the southern suburbs, in which the Slaters located, is a visual delight, whether by night or by day. Though Slater deeply loved Grahamstown, Alice, and the Amatola Mountains of his youth and early life, he must have found joy and rest at Manystairs.

Evidence of what Cape Town, at least in part, did for him lies in the fact that he left Grahamstown an ill and exhausted man. In his new home he was to have granted twenty-seven more years, years used to focus and conclude what he had started even as a boy.

III *Travel*

In South Africa long leave has always been used for travel. One might even say that it was provided to make travel possible. Slater availed himself of these opportunities and had for twenty-five years been making trips to England and the Continent, the intention being to go every five years. Now, however, travel could be more leisurely and at times which suited his convenience. It is also obvious that finally places other than Europe could be considered, and a few were actually visited. During 1933 he and his wife selected Victoria Falls, the Matoppos, and the Zimbabwe Ruins—in Southern Rhodesia. Today air travel makes this a simple trip from Cape Town, but in the 1930's it was more than sixteen hundred miles by rail to Victoria.

Discovered by Dr. David Livingstone on November 16, 1855, Victoria Falls had attracted visitors from faraway lands. At last Slater was turning his attention to the things of his own part of the world; that is, to things which did not mean home, or the Amatola Hills, the Keiskama, or the Drakensberg. Victoria was, of course, a natural wonder, worthy of attention for itself alone. Before the falls one need only stand in human awe. This is precisely what Slater did, as the long train ride came to an end.

> Gazing ahead I saw tall vapour-spires
> Rising like smoke from angry forest-fires:
> —That is the 'smoke that thunders,' this my Inn:
> Here eager journeys end: wonders begin!
>
> Mountains are bubbles to that voice whose roar
> Dims that of many oceans merged in one;
> Drawn by its magnet-might I hurried on
> Until I reached at last the shaken shore.
> Forgotten then the weariness of long leagues travelled:
> Dust were past dreams and mist each travel-story;
> The knotted skein of distance and unravelled,
> I saw Zambesi in his magnitude and glory.
> I saw the wild trees dance, the mad rocks leap

Against behemoth-heave and lightning-sweep
Of water down bewildered precipices
Into fiend-racked abysses.
And from the tumult of that seething cauldron
Swift, silvery vapours rose,
Girdled with iridescent bows,
To hail the harping sun.
Yes, then I saw Zambesi's leaping flocks,
Bearded Angora rams with sweeping locks,
Curled snow-white fleeces streaked with gold,
Ten million in a moment flashed,
Ten million in a moment crashed
To the rapacious fold.[2]

Seeking out the Zimbabwe Ruins was for the purpose of allowing man to look upon creations of man. Though the site must have been known to the Portuguese, the official date of discovery is that made by a hunter, Adam Render, in 1868. Scientific investigation suggests that the ruins are perhaps something over a thousand years old and are Bantu. Everything is of stone construction, great granite blocks fitted without mortar. There is no evidence of roofing at any period. The Acropolis, probably for defense, stands on a three-hundred-and-fifty-foot granite hill. A second area is the Valley of the Ruins, but the most interesting discovery was the Temple, built as an irregular ellipse, three hundred and fifty feet across, with walls up to thirty-four feet and with a thickness of as much as sixteen feet at the bottom and of ten feet at the top. Many relics have been discovered, despite prescientific-period ransacking by treasure hunters. It is estimated that a thousand ounces of gold were stolen, mostly in the form of ornaments; much of it was melted down, and thus its historical value was lost. Many gold or iron ornaments, however, were discovered at later dates, along with Persian pottery, Arab glass, and imported porcelain. Despite all that has been identified and decided by experts, one of the attractions of Zimbabwe is the mystery which still surrounds these ancient stones, metals, and all that has been located. Slater could not have been unmoved, though he did not attempt to record his feelings in verse.

Any man might be expected to wish to see Victoria Falls and the Zimbabwe Ruins, but Slater had very personal reasons for his visit to the Matoppos. It was here that Cecil Rhodes was buried. Rhodes had died in Muizenberg on March 26, 1902. After services in Cape Town, his body was taken in his own railway car on the long, last ride to the Matoppos, of which in his will he had said, "I admire the grandeur and loneliness of the Matoppos, and therefore I desire to be buried in the Matoppos on the hill which I used to visit and which I called the 'View of the World' in a square to be cut in the rock. . . ." Upon a gun carriage drawn by oxen, his coffin was taken up the black slope of the hill, a slope swarming with Matabele, who cried, "Our father is dead!" Rhodes only among white men, before or since, they gave the royal salute, "*Bayete!*" It was this sound that echoed from the "World View" rather than the usual rifle salute because the Matabele indunas (headmen) feared that the noise of guns might disturb the spirits of departed Matabele chiefs believed to dwell in a small cave nearby. Thus, upon the 4,700-foot-hill called Malindidzimu, he who could never rest was brought to a final rest.

In 1898 Slater had composed a blank-verse tribute to Rhodes, lines sent to and acknowledged by Rhodes himself. This effort was included in Slater's first volume but not thereafter. It was at the time of Rhodes's death that Slater wrote what he considered worthy of being preserved among the final selection of his work. Here he began his commemoration with lines which identified the burial place.

> In the Matoppos now he lies,
>   Where warm winds fret;
> His bouldered hills, his burning skies
>   Are near him yet.[3]

Having waited thirty years, Slater now stood upon those bouldered hills and let his mind drift back to Rhodes, who had died younger than Slater at the time of this visit.

Still in his twenties, long before his marriage, Slater had made his first trip to England and the Continent. Now, however, not yet sixty, he with his wife left Cape Town for what once was called the Grand Tour, a trip needing months and covering many countries. After some weeks in what he termed "irresistible London," the Slaters started for Paris, Geneva, Milan, and Venice. Florence was next and detained the travelers for two weeks. From Florence they went to Pisa.

While he was viewing buildings, statues, and paintings, Francis Carey Slater was a man of few words. If any of these things, however, had been associated with a person he valued, his whole approach changed. The following example will make clear his practice:

We took a taxi at Pisa and motored to San Torenzio, on the bay of Lerici, in order to see Shelley's last home, the Casa Magni. We ran into some heavy showers along the way, but were not to be deterred from our quest. When we reached the Casa Magni, we found it shut. I walked along to a cottage hard by, whose owner told me that the caretaker of the place had gone off to visit a friend—the retainer of a grandee living three or four miles from the village. As he offered to guide us, we took him along. The grandee's house was an imposing mansion situated in large grounds full of ornamental trees, among which gleamed many white marble statues. Here, we soon discovered the absconding caretaker, and hauled him back with us to the village. The Casa Magni is a solid building based upon rock formations jutting into the bay of Lerici. The upper floor, once occupied by the Shelleys, consists of one large room and four smaller ones. A door from the large living-room opens on to a wide upper-veranda, or balcony, floored with stone, and overlooking the sea. In stormy weather this veranda must, I imagine, have been frequently splashed by the spray of wind-swept waves. Articles of furniture in the house are said to be those used by the Shelleys. The caretaker and our taximan followed us about whilst we went through the premises. When our inspection was over the caretaker enquired of us, in broken English, where we came from. When I replied, "South Africa," the two worthies gazed at each other in bewilderment. At last one of them exclaimed triumphantly, "In-de-a!" When I tried to explain the entire difference of locality involved, they were again puzzled; but what they thoroughly understood and appreciated were the tips which came their way later. Upon our return run along the Bay of Spezzia, we paused to examine the small stone-pillar marking the spot on the sands where Shelley's body was burnt. At Viareggio we stopped to see his beautiful marble monument. Has Italy realized the splendour of Shelley's genius more truly than has the land of his birth?[4]

From Pisa the travelers moved on to Rome, Naples, Bari, and thence to Athens. From Athens they passed through the Gulf of Corinth into the Ionian Sea and on into the Adriatic and, among other places, viewed the island of Corfu. Too many places were visited to name all, but Belgrade and Budapest were among them. In speaking of Vienna, Slater pauses to remark upon members of the world of music associated with the city and names an opera seen while there. Prague was next, and then the couple moved rapidly on to end their European sojourn in Brussels.

It was in 1938 that Slater and his wife made a last visit to England, to which this time they added Norway. As always, London was included during the English stay. On this trip he especially mentions going to Tintern Abbey and comments upon Wordsworth's poem, which is associated with the Wye. Stonehenge also was included, but he seems to have been more impressed by a "choir of larks" than by the circular group of stones. Making his fourth appearance at Oxford, he saw his old friend, R. C. K. Ensor, of Corpus Christi. Here he met H. W. Garrod, Edmund Blunden, and Sir Richard Livingstone. Ensor and Blunden were to aid Slater in the publication of his first "collected" volume, 1947.

When he was into his seventies, Slater made a second pilgrimage into Southern Rhodesia. The account given suggests that he and his wife found the eastern side of the country visually more inviting than sixteen years earlier they had found the western. He speaks of motoring to Inyanga "amid scenes of wild grandeur"—an area offering the highest peak in the country, 8,517 feet. From Inyanga they drove on through the Vumba Hills, rising to 5,000 feet, twenty miles from Umtali, where they took a train down to Beira to sail from there back to the Cape, on his return after the immediate business of his visit had been completed.

In early childhood Slater seems to have been moved by natural beauty, and this capacity for deep reaction seems never to have deserted him. Yet the reason for what became the last visit to Southern Rhodesia was to meet a man with whom he had been corresponding for almost thirty years. This was the now blind and almost deaf poet-missionary Arthur Shearly Cripps. In *The Centenary Book of South African Verse* (1925), Slater had used fifteen of Cripps's poems and considered him one of the best poets living in Africa—an accurate estimate. The two men had never met. From Cape Town Slater had made the voyage round the east coast of Africa, had gone inland by train to Umtali, then by car ninety-two miles south to Enkeldoorn.

Very early in the twentieth century, Arthur Shearly Cripps, as he was entering his thirties, left England in November, 1900, and reached Africa at Beira on January 3, 1901. He traveled inland to Umtali, where an old friend had charge of the parish. The still youthful Cripps remained for several weeks, and here he met another man who has written African poems of importance. Cripps left a record of this encounter: "I remember Kingsley Fairbridge at Umtali in 1901; he was by way of adventuring there, if I remember aright, as a market-gardener with a partner much older than himself; he was a fair-haired, fresh-coloured, eager boy of fifteen."[5] The two men, however, were moving in different directions, Fairbridge toward becoming Africa's first Rhodes Scholar and Cripps one of the most distinctive missionaries of the century.

During March Cripps went further into the interior, to the open plains of the Charter district. He learned the Shona language, and here he acquired land. On a farm, six miles from Enkeldoorn, he built his hut and his church. He named the station Maronda Mashanu—the mission of the Five Wounds. There he lived, except for short periods and one break of almost four years (1926-30) until his death in 1952.[6] This little mission, with Cripps quite literally its heart and soul, for fifty years endured without assistance from either church or state.[7] Along with the spiritual strength which poured from Maronda Mashanu came poem after poem of indisputable authenticity. It was this man and his work that brought an admirer on the journey from the Cape. Slater seems to have found in Cripps all he expected and to have departed with a feeling of deep satisfaction.

Very few things that Slater did or remarked upon reveal more about him than his travels and the various comments upon what he saw and heard. It appears that he had little of the spirit of adventure. Seldom does he seem to have visited places for any delights he might discover, but he always went because of what he expected to find, even for what he felt sure was present.

Last Prose Stories, The Secret Veld, *1931*

W RITING a novel apparently turned Slater's mind again in the direction of prose fiction. Eighteen years had passed since his first collection of stories had been published. Now during 1926 and 1927 he wrote a number of short narratives for magazine use. In 1931 he made his final collection of short fiction under the title *The Secret Veld,* a volume containing all seven stories, revised, from *The Sunburnt South,* and nine new stories. The author reports that the book was well received by the press but that sales were only moderate. He explains that publishers and booksellers told him that readers preferred novels to collections of short stories. This is with little doubt true. Hereafter he published no more short stories, which is unfortunate, since *The Secret Veld* is one of his most successful books.

From the beginning, Slater's titles had suggested South Africa—the land itself and its history. Before publication of *The Secret Veld,* he had made no attempt to explain the implications of the words and phrases used. This volume offered a long preface in which he not only explains the meaning of "veld" in its South African setting but also suggests how all of this detailed fact presents a symbol of what he was trying to achieve in his book.

The "Veld" is the general term used in South Africa to denote open country. It is a fairly elastic term and embraces karroo-veld, grass-veld, berg-veld, low-veld, high-veld, and so on. A somewhat comprehensive description of the karroo-veld will be found in the first chapter of one of the following stories, *The Minstrel.* From this it may be seen that, in times of drought, and when scourged by the noon-day sun, the karroo can appear as harsh, repellent, and hideous as a basking crocodile; that in the rare, rainy seasons it burgeons into radiant beauty beneath a million, million minute and lovely wild-flowers; that at sunrise and sunset it can become more

gorgeous than the most splendid fabrics woven in the looms of the imagination, and that, beneath the benign influence of the moonlight it glimmers
with the mystical and tender loveliness of fairyland.

Now he presents details which identify the various kinds of veld.

As for grass-veld, we have the undulating hills of the Eastern Province
clothed with red-brown grass and dotted with golden-balled mimosa-
thorn: the low, billowy, grass-glad hills of Pondoland, dappled with lovely
little groves of yellowwood trees—fragments of more extensive forests of
former years; and we have the long, level, monotonous grass-covered plains
of the Orange Free State.

For bush-veld. we have the country so inimitably described in that veld-
classic, *Jock of the Bushveld*. . . .

But, even as in the case of our karroo-veld, we have much in our bush-
veld that is harsh, repellent and unlovely. In the neighbourhood of the
Great Fish River there are miles upon square-miles of dwarfish bush, scaly
cacti, flabby-leaved prickly-pear and countless grovelling, serpent-like
plants. Here, too, are huge groves of the weird and ghostly euphorbia tree.

Our berg-veld is equally varied. We have the bold, bald-topped
mountains of the Western Province which frequently display such startingly
lovely opalescent and shell-pink effects at dawn and at sunset. Then we
have the Drakensberg . . . which, for sublime scenery, are the chief glory of
South Africa. We have also the Amatola Hills, which—rising like blue
dreams in the distance—are more beautiful than the visions of a poet when
you approach them and climb their magical slopes.

Following all of this classification, he offers his emotional reaction
and then comments upon the relation between his stories and the
veld he has discussed.

Thus our veld scenery can be lovely, radiant, and sublime; harsh,
repellent and hideous; kindly, open and candid; and taciturn, sinister and
secret. . . .It has, doubtless, many other qualities and attributes, but a
concatenation of adjectives will not serve to pluck the heart from the
"secret veld".

The characteristics of the veld are to some extent reflected in the character of its inhabitants. Many of these are simple and kindly and as open
and candid as a sun-flooded plain covered with honest grass. Others are
endowed with darker traits: they are subtle, secretive, acquisitive and
quarrelsome. Bitter race-hatreds and virulent political animosities have
rendered them incapable of seeing the other fellow's side of a question,
or of playing the game.[1]

Not only the characters but the stories of the volume are as varied as the veld. There is the visionary account of a poet's progress through life, merged with an idealized love; yet this may be contrasted with the tale of a man who peddled cabbage. Then there is the story of a bank clerk who was dominated by his mother and later by his wife and his daughter but who with great courage opposed armed robbers; this can be contrasted with the encounter of a native minister, converted to Christianity, and yet having to deal with the African belief in "Hili." The differences continue as story after story is read.

I *The Use of Personal Experiences*

How closely associated with his raw material Slater could become is demonstrated by identifying the situation from which germinated the story he called "The Red Maiden" in 1908 and "The Dictionary" in 1931. In his autobiography when he recalls his school days at Lovedale, he speaks of the impact of European dress upon the students.

. . . Most of the [male pupils] wore plain European garments. But there was amongst them a sprinkling of dandies, who disdained the commonplace. These usually wore short tightly fitting black or dark coats, trousers of some light check material, tight at the knees and so wide at the ankles as almost to conceal black brightly-polished, high-heeled boots: white starched shirts, with the highest stand-up collars procurable, and ties of the most startling tint and hue imaginable. They wore soft felt hats, around which brightly-coloured tasselled silk-scarves were so cunningly wound as to give the tassels free play over one of the ears of the wearer. These dandies walked about in a solemn dignified manner, bringing their high-heeled boots down with audible thuds, which to them doubtless represented a musical accompaniment to motion. . . . Their favourite study . . . was the English Dictionary. They poured over this in order to cull from it the longest and most sonorous words they could find. They made lists of these words—or "tearms," as they called them—and carefully incorporated certain of the more formidable of them in their school-compositions and private letters. . . .[2]

When the author introduces Moses Mpondo, he is dressed precisely as described in the autobiography. The young Bantu student at the Mission Station school is preparing a recitation for the commencement exercises. Moses is fourth on the program. He proceeds, on the occasion, to the platform and announces that he will recite "Leetle Geem." Without a pause he completes the first stanza and then discovers that he has forgotten the second. Thus he returns to the first. After the rendering of the initial line, his memory fails to produce the next line. Again he attacks the opening line, only to go blank in the middle. By this time he has his audience thoroughly entertained, but for the wrong reason. Whereupon he turns to the chairman with the observation, "The paradoxical demonstration of stupendous redundancy is unmitigated by despicable degeneration."[3] The audience cheers, and Moses, rather satisfied with himself, returns to his seat.

In this state he goes back to his home, where his "words" make him a distinct success. Here the account could end. This, however, would be an episode, not a short story. Thus, all that has happened becomes an introduction to the story which is developing.

Soon after he reaches home, Moses, with his dictionary, goes out for a walk and encounters a girl who upsets his poise. When she asks the meaning of the book, he replies, "Stupendous, unmitigated fascination." She requests an explanation and is told it says *she is a pretty girl*. Fascination in both directions develops rapidly, but trouble is close. Two men appear and start to "carry" the girl Maliwe. Here again Slater offers an example of the Bantu custom of Uku Twala. (See pp. 37-38.) Maliwe, however, objects to being carried. She wants Moses, who has said he will go to work in the mines to secure money for *lobola*, a kind of dowry. Though her chosen man has no chance against two men armed with kerries, he trails her and that night with a well-thought-out and well-executed plan he rescues her. They elope, *Uku gcagca*, and find work far away. The "Stupendous, unmitigated fascination" becomes effective for many years.

Growing directly out of the author's mature personal life as "The Dictionary" had from his youthful experiences, "Wonderful Women" should be considered for the idea it quite explicitly offers. Very early the narrator insists that his story "serves to show how a man—regarded by his fellows as a nonentity and a coward—may, when put to the test, reveal astounding courage."[4] He illustrates his claim by revealing the life of a man who had been completely dominated by his mother, whom he always referred to as a "wonderful woman." Following his mother's death, he married (or was married by) a woman older than he, who ruled him totally. He always spoke of her, too, as a "wonderful woman." After a number of years, she died; yet by this time there was a grown daughter (also a "wonderful woman") who handled her father in the same manner as that employed by wife and mother. During all of these years, he had returned at night to the bank, where he was a clerk, for the expressed purpose of checking his work for the day. He did do the announced checking, and his accounts were always correct the following day; yet as the years passed, it became obvious that he went to the bank to avoid his "wonderful women."

Because he always returned to the bank, he is there one night when armed robbery is attempted by three men. His action, even after he is shot through the shoulder, shows him to be a man of courage and daring. Everyone is now able to see that this quiet little man has another side, one they had never guessed.

Briefly, in 1906, Slater had been sent to the Grahamstown branch of the Standard Bank. Then in 1917 he had returned as its manager. His own banking movements are made to serve as the structure of the time and setting of the story. Here is how he begins to build his narrative.

"A good many years ago I was sent to relieve the teller at the Saintsbury branch of the Southern Star Banking Company. By the way, have you ever been to Saintsbury? No? Well, you've something to live for.

"Saintsbury is the most English town I have seen out of England; it is a sedate and stately old city. It is situated in a cup-like recess, surrounded by undulating hills. It has clean, wide streets, lined with oak and Kaffir-boom and studded with small, oval-shaped islands clothed with grass and ornamental trees.

"It has a dignified cathedral and two or three beautiful churches whose lofty spires flame to the farewell gestures of the sun. It has several college buildings, of grey stone and slate roof that might almost have come out of Oxford. It has a Supreme Court (an architectural monstrosity—one of the few blots in an otherwise beautiful town). . . .

"It has enchanting public gardens where Nature and Art have met altogether, loveliness and tranquility have kissed each other. Here you may wander from trim lawns and a shady oak-avenue to a hillside fane dotted with altars of grey rock lit up by the flaming candles of the wild aloe. . . ."[5]

The detailed accuracy of all of this is attested by the author's copying or paraphrasing sections from his stories when as an elderly man he came to the writing of an autobiography. In presenting this fact, there is no intention of claiming that the method makes the stories (or the novel before them) more effective, or less effective, but to establish the authenticity of the materials for a new generation of readers, many of them thousands of miles away from the original source. A reader is being given what was in South Africa at that time.

II *Intensely African Stories*

Several other stories make one aware of being in South Africa. The most intense awareness emerges from an account of the small native boy who was interested in art. This story, reprinted in *The Secret Veld*, was discussed in Chapter 3, see pp. 29-30. Likewise one has a strong sense of Africa in the presentation of the man who with his hands kills the leopard who had taken the life of the girl he loves. A struggle between an older Africa and a new one attempting to come into existence is found in the story which the author called "Hili." He had first approached this native belief in verse for a 1910 volume and again in verse in 1935, the same material revised. (See pp. 38 and pp. 120-121). In a prose story his use of the belief shows him attempting a very different result.

New Africa is represented by the Reverend Nicodemus Tuta and old Africa by the Reverend Samuel Magaba. Tuta assumes that he has discarded what he now considers the superstitious Bantu belief in Hili, or Tekoloshe; thus he is disappointed and even angry when he receives a letter from Magaba warning him that the woman Nompata, now his housekeeper, "is a bad woman. It is said that she 'has Hili' and that he visits her at night. It is also said that she poisoned her husband because he found out about her Hili."[6] Tuta ponders the letter in disgust and despair.

". . . Samuel, an educated man—a minister—talking about witchcraft and Hili! Hili, indeed! I am ashamed of Samuel. It seems useless trying to raise these people. In spite of all our preaching and teaching, they cling to their heathenish superstitions! It is discouraging—very discouraging."[7]

Despite his scorn of Bantu superstition, Tuta does not sleep well that night. About midnight he awakens conscious in a vague way of a window being opened and closed. Then he dozes off again. Later he is awakened by the same kind of sound. He rises, but an inspection of the house reveals nothing. This is repeated the next night. A call at Nompata's door brings the reply that she has heard nothing. The next evening Tuta summons the woman to his study and tells her it has been said that she "had Hili." She answers "Yes" and admits that it visits her and had done so the previous night and was with her when he came to the door. She explains that she refused to allow him to enter because it would have caused his death. He insists that he does not believe in Hili and that she *must* call him upon another visit. She agrees. Next day she admits being visited but pleads that she was afraid to call.

The heathen traditions of his boyhood were spreading their tentacles around him again. Against the prompting of his better nature, he was imperceptibly drifting into the superstitions he had scoffed at for years and preached against with withering scorn and contempt. But notwithstanding the grisly doubts that now assailed him, he determined to see the matter through.[8]

Thus, he demands that she call him if there is another appearance. She agrees.

Toward midnight, Tuta is roused by the woman's call. He lights a candle and goes, finding her scantily dressed, sitting upon the side of her bed, and in seeming terror.

Tuta glanced quickly from the woman to the window. The sash of this was slightly raised and rested upon a brick that lay lengthwise across the sill. A dark green blind covered the window and rested, somewhat crinkled, upon the brick. Seeing nothing to account for the woman's terrified appearance, Tuta turned towards her to seek some explanation. She had risen from the bed in the meantime, and had approached him. Suddenly she flung her arms around him and whispered tensely:

"Umfundisi, I am afraid. I am afraid!"

He felt her tremble and tighten her clasp; he heard her heart beat; her warm breath was upon his face; her hot eyes gleamed into his.

Still dull and heavy from sleep, he had been taken completely unawares. His heart-beats quickened; his mouth became parched, and a choking sensation clutched his throat. The beast within him—the grim monster he had conquered and crushed—gripped him suddenly with irresistible force. The candle dropped from his hand and went out: the room was now in total darkness. The woman clung closer to him: her body burned against his like a devouring flame. Scarcely realising what he did, his arms enfolded her savagely and his thirsty lips sought hers.

At this moment, he was suddenly arrested by a noise at the window: the sash was raised gently and the blind rustled. A cold puff of air invaded the room, accompanied—it seemed to him—by a nauseous odour of stagnant water. The window-blind rustled again. Then he heard a stealthy, almost noiseless tread upon the floor. He felt his hair stir suddenly; a cold sweat bedewed his brow. In a flash he remembered the woman's words: "Umfundisi, he will kill you: he will cause your death as he did that of my husband." Overcome with sudden unreasoning terror, he flung the woman from him roughly and rushed out.[9]

Soon after dawn, the woman comes to his door, bringing coffee. Through the locked door he orders her to leave his house. As the conversation proceeds, she reveals much by her "I like you much better than—" Finally, Tuta challenges her with "Would you poison me as you did your husband?"[10] There is a gasp, the crash of a cup, and retreating steps. Soon afterward the front door slams, and he sees the woman going toward the river. At the river she changes from European to native dress and moves up the valley.

Gazing after the woman, Tuta saw, or imagined he saw, a dim grey object—a shadowless shadow—following her. He rubbed his sun-dazzled eyes and stared intently and wonderingly: was it—could it be—Hili? Or was it an emanation of evil—the hideous nature of the woman divorced for a moment from her beautiful body?
The window behind Tuta opened suddenly, causing him to start violently. The black tom-cat, Ntsundu, leaped from the window-sill and rubbed himself fondly against his master's legs.
Blessed illumination came to Tuta in a lightning flash. He stooped down, and, stroking Ntsundu's silky coat, murmured in solemn ecstasy:
"Out of Darkness cometh Light!"[11]

In this short story, Slater has done what earlier he had in verse—shown that Bantu belief was founded on fact, not imagination. What he allows the reader to see is a natural explanation of what had by natives been described in supernatural terms.
How completely Slater could localize an ancient theme is seen in "Soete Aapie," a story in which a father, without knowing what he is doing, kills a son. The tragic climax is the recognition scene. Stretching more than two thousand years back of the author was the Greek myth of Oedipus, used again and again from Sophocles down to the twentieth century. Likewise, there are parallels, also appearing through the centuries. In the nineteenth century there

is the well-known "Sohrab and Rustum" of Matthew Arnold, the story of a Persian hero who in ignorance of the warrior's identity kills his son in single combat. Using the theme in still another way, this time very close to the approach employed by the South African author, the twentieth-century American poet Robert Penn Warren relates how a father in ignorance of a traveler's identity kills his son.[12] As was often true in ancient stories, both Warren and Slater use a physical characteristic of the son in the recognition scene. Both also make the narrative one which emerges from the place and time in which it is set.

In a horseshoe of the Bushman's River in the Cape Province of South Africa lived Piet Pienaar, his wife Katrina, and one child, young Piet. There is Jantje, an aged Hottentot servant, and Marta, a nursemaid. The story begins when old Jantje reports that the baboons are in the mealie lands. Piet says that he will get his gun and have a shot at the intruders into his growing corn. Jantje advises shooting over the baboons because "They are but people." Piet scoffs at the idea and proceeds toward the fields with his gun. Suddenly a hiss warns him of a puff adder which his short-sighted eyes failed to detect. Sufficiently warned, he stones the snake to death and moves past the poisonous menace. As he approaches the fields, he notices movement within the expanse of green. He fires. There is a sudden scurry, and he rushes forward and fires again. A scream follows, as of an infant in pain. Then Piet finds himself confronted by a large grey baboon. Out of cartridges, he grasps his gun and prepares to fight for his life. The baboon stops, and Piet sees a baby baboon at the father's feet, the small one evidently near death. The father lifts the baby and disappears among the mealies.

Afterward in telling his wife of the events, Piet laments his actions and observes how tragic it would be to him if anything should happen to their child, little Piet, "*soete aapie*," sweet little ape. Whereupon his father takes the child in his arms and remarks upon his one blue eye and one brown eye, a characteristic seldom offered by nature, but taken by the mother as a symbol of the union of her brown eyes with her husband's blue.

That afternoon, trustingly, father and mother make a trip to the *dorp*, town, and leave little Piet in the care of Marta. When Marta takes the child out for his usual afternoon walk, they stop for a rest. Little Piet drops off to sleep and Marta does likewise.

Awakened by a thunderstorm, Marta finds the child gone and runs screaming in search of little Piet, just as his parents are returning from the town. The search, continued through the night, is in vain. The child is never found.

Years later the reader again sees Jantje, now reputed to be over a hundred, approach and report that the baboons are in the mealie lands. When again Piet says he will shoot them, Jantje requests that he desist, that he shoot over them, because they "are but people." As before, however, Piet goes with his gun. Approaching the mealie fields, he sees two baboons coming toward him. Peering through his short-sighted eyes, hurriedly he fires. One baboon falls with a scream. Going up to the creature now quivering in death, Piet looks down upon two glazing eyes, one brown and one blue.

Here is perhaps the most directly narrated and unadorned story of Slater's career. He has merely presented the incidents and allowed the reader to decide how he feels. The author has learned to trust the action of his narrative.

Handling very different raw material in "The Mermaid," he offers evidence of his ability to create what Edgar Allan Poe called the necessary or at least desirable "pre-conceived effect" of the short-story form. Slater is writing a story of mystery and horror and trying to create maximum suspense.

Starting with the affirmation by Mr. Lustrefield, a farmer living some miles from the mouth of the Kesi River, in the Eastern Province of the Cape, South Africa, that he has seen a mermaid among the rushes of a small island across a deep pool of considerable length, the story continues with speculation upon alternative theories to explain what was actually seen. Action follows theory; tempo and tension increase steadily; the climax is definite—giving an answer to the mystery—and the story is terminated immediately without one word of author interference for comment.

As might be expected, the solution reached depends on natural rather than on supernatural causes. Though the stories have nothing in common otherwise, this one fact connects "The Mermaid" with "Hili." (See pp. 110-112.)

III   *Something Dear to the Author*

Among the sixteen stories which Slater published in *The Secret Veld*, he probably revealed more of himself in "The Minstrel" than in anything else he wrote as short fiction. Here he preserved his final effort to capture in prose the spirit of the Karroo. Here is found his most complete effort to present his concept of feminine childhood. Here, too, is seen his most intense effort to depict what he considered the steadfastness of the feminine nature. Here he brings his chief characters to South Africa to find a solution to their problems. Obviously, this story is very much a part of the author's inner world.

Yet nothing mentioned above is at the center of the story nor the heart of Slater's life. That honor is held by the principle character's dream of becoming a poet. What is being implied is not that the author makes himself a character in the story. The action of Laurence Selden does not imitate the action of Francis Carey Slater. The implication is much deeper. From childhood young Francis must have yearned for poethood. By the age of eight he was made aware of some of the powers of poetry and seems to have begun searching his environment for possible materials as subject matter for his verses. At almost no time in his conscious life was he without thoughts of poetry and of becoming a poet. The examples which had introduced him to a world of art were always from far away, usually from England. Thus, poetry must often have been something to dream about. Yet he early attempted to make the dreams into verses. Gradually he was accepted. Therefore, when he came to the end of a long life, he looked back upon the years through a collection of books covering half a century. Slater could hardly have made a poet the chief character of a story without thinking of himself and of his own writing.

Perhaps even more important than the creation of the principal character of the story is the fourteen-page section in which he attempts to present the life of a poet and show how his influence is felt throughout the world. Yet, as the years pass and the poet moves on, he realizes his inability to achieve what he had dreamed —the actual never equals his vision. He considers himself a failure, but to the world he does not abandon his songs of hope. As old age approaches and death is near, the poet climbs a mountain from which he discovers he can look upon the scenes of his childhood. Gazing upon the valley of his youth, he experiences again the vision of those early days. The day ends, his life ends, "and he was alone with the stars."[13]

In addition to his dreaming, his idealism, and his visionary technique in presenting the poet's journey through life, Slater gives all of this an elaborate local setting for a frame. Laurence Selden, the living poet who is in the action from beginning to end, is introduced as he sees the Karroo while crossing the area by train. Throughout the night he journeys alone, but during the next morning a girl of about ten, Linda Summers, on the way to school, enters his compartment. Through their conversation, Selden discovers that Linda's teacher from England is the love of his youth. In the tradition of romantic fiction, she has waited for him. That evening Selden visits Miss Stanley's cottage, and the usual conclusion ensues.

This story, written and first published in 1908, represents attitudes and ideas which the author was unwilling to abandon in 1931. It should be remembered, however, that in this volume he includes everything from the early collection, not merely "The Minstrel." The significant thing to observe is the improvement made between the early and late stories, represented not only by the new compositions but by the revisions made in the early ones.

Youth Revisited, Dark Folk, *1935*

NEAR the end of 1931 Slater and his wife made the important decision to leave the Eastern Province, where they had spent most of their years, and settle in Cape Town. In this new environment Francis Carey Slater began to relive and rethink the first half of his life. He culled, revised, and rewrote his early lines and continued his devotion to South African poetry by reconsidering completely the *Centenary Book.* Finally, looking back over his life and the history of his land, he made two of his most important contributions to the literature of his country—*Dark Folk and Other Poems* and *The Trek.* The first emerges from his own life; the second from the life of the Dutch segment of the South African population.

I *Lines That Time Made*

Often passage of time and separation by space are necessary before one can attain the poise which makes possible the writing of which a given individual is capable. When Slater moved to Manystairs and commenced his walks through Wynberg Park, going on up the hill beyond, and finally into and along Rhodes Drive, he began to drift back forty to fifty years in memory and in imagination to span hundreds of miles. Many of the "Dark Folk" units had been written and published years earlier. Now the whole was organized. These lines offered his understanding of the Xhosas, one of the greatest of the Bantu tribes, with whom he had associated as a child. Now looking back he told in elegiacs the story of his early reading. To this period belongs "The Settlers' Churchyard," a statement of his admiration for the lives of the English pioneers and what they contributed to the development of South Africa. Three times he introduced into this volume lines about Hogsback, the mountain peak which captured his imagination during the days of his youth in Alice. The climax of the book comes in "The Dead Eagle." In 1957 Roy Campbell said that nothing greater had been written in South Africa. Many readers felt that this 1935 publication was his most important volume.

Introducing the "Dark Folk" section, Slater admitted that because there was no worthy volume of Xhosa poems he was tempted to write one and then make a translation. Instead he offered openly an interpretation of the life and attitudes of people he knew well. Regardless of how accurate and intimate the presentation of Xhosa life is, the mind which presents this material is a European-trained intelligence, not a primitive Xhosa consciousness. Slater, however, because of his extremely special position and knowledge, probably has been able to bring an English audience as close to actuality as it is possible to get. Indeed, a reader may understand more from that which is written from his own point of reference than an alien one.

Studying the "Dark Folk" collection as a whole, a reader begins to understand general characteristics in addition to acquiring detailed facts. Very quickly he will see that it is the outdoor world to which the Xhosa mind clings, not the indoor world. Likewise, it is the world of light upon which attention focuses, not the world of darkness. Soon it is evident that thought often turns toward food, though extremely simple—essentially milk and mealies. Work assumes a very prominent place in the Xhosa day, three tasks being dominant—hoeing the mealies, herding, and milking the cows. Having been established, any characteristic can be very easily emphasized by its absence. Thus, when a man is required by circumstances to enter the mines, his concern is for the loss of sunlight, the out-of-doors, and of his milk, mealies, and cattle.

How important cattle are to the Xhosas can be determined by the frequency with which they appear, not only as the subject, but incidentally, and by the significance of the context in which they are present. Exclusive of their great value because of the food they supply, cattle become involved in ritual and are the basis for calculating wealth and establishing social position.

Quantity is not always needed to establish general actions, attitudes, or concepts. Often one title is enough. Initiation into manhood is presented in "Abekweta Dance"; use of a Bantu tradition in "Hili's Bride"; dangers from snakes in "Langa's Lament for Lila." The author is perhaps coming closest to native actuality in the various chants, such as "Vuku," a Xhosa morning song; "Xhosa Roadmenders Chant"; and "Hoeing Chant."

In addition to all that is successful because it is descriptive or expository, though these lines are ultimately symbolic, Slater's best work in the "Dark Folk" collection is that which is concerned with an individual and thus can become dramatic. "Mandi" is based on the report of a trial for murder, in the circuit court at Butterworth, in the Transkei. Mandi loved and expected to marry young Kumbula. One day while she was hoeing her father's mealies, Bombo took her bound to his hut. That night he overcame and violated her. Next day she noticed a hatchet close by. This she hid under her blanket. That night when she again resisted him, he started to strike as before. Mandi struck first. Bombo fell across red embers and never rose from his fall. At the trial Mandi told the complete story to the judge and jury. After the deliberation of the jury, the judge pronounced the sentence: "Mandi . . . you are not guilty. . . ."

> The prisoner gulped and stuttered:
> "What? Not to die? Not dangle on a dead tree?
> Greetings and thanks unto the king upon the high seat!
> I am bewildered! Ask him, see he rises,
> Since Bombo's dead, who now will pay the cattle,
> As compensation to my father for the damage
> The dead man did to me? I am bewildered!
> He goes! He has not said who'll pay the cattle!
> I am bewildered. . . . Who will pay the cattle?"[1]

These lines tell more about the Xhosa attitude toward lobola, the cattle given as a dowry, than many pages of factual explanation. Inextricably entangled with the concept of the lobola are the mental processes of the Xhosa. In Mandi's civilization, the place filled by lobola is so profound that she cannot conceive of any situation in which its absence may be permitted. To attribute this to naïveté, simple-mindedness, or anything of the kind, is undoubtedly to miss the whole point. Up to this exclamation, Mandi has been characterized as completely normal in every way. It would seem proper to say that here the reader has seen dramatically rendered action and attitude which offer the very essence of a civilization.

Most of the substance which served as raw material for the Dark

003

12   FRANCIS CAREY SLATER

Folk series was factual and available to Slater because of direct
contacts during childhood and youth. Raw materials, however, do
not create anything, either good or bad. Authors create. In "Hili's
Bride" Slater starts with an old Bantu tradition or superstition
concerning Hili or Tekoloshe. As raw material this is almost completely inert, yet Slater has used it in the development of an
extremely effective tragedy. He starts with the lament of a maid
destined to wed an old man on the morrow.

> Mated with a greybeard, while through me like a hill-torrent
> Youth crashes, heat tingles as sap in a shooting tree.[2]

Unable to sleep, the maid rises from her bed and passes "into the
largeness of the night," eventually finding herself stopped by
"the dark sweeping river." Trembling "above star-stippled water,"
she hears "singing from below." It is Hili's invitation: "Come into
the water and live with me,/Earth's lovely daughter, virginal and
free."[3] The maid accepts the invitation,but then it becomes Hili's
turn to lament. Long before now, of course, a reader knows literally
what is happening.

> Late last night I was wakened from my sleep,
> By a dead-white, sullen moon with dagger-glancing beams,
> A swarthy maiden stood by the star-shot river-side
> And wept as she watched its dappled waters flow.
> Lithe as a leopardess and lovely as a tree,
> She swayed on the river-bank among the feathered reeds,
> Lovely as a leopardess she glowed among the rushes,
> And weeping watched the python-stream hissing gleam and glide.
> Hesitant she lingered there, vestured by the moon,
> While I panted forth my passion in a star-delighting song . . .
> She came to me, sad Hili, long doomed to live alone! . . .
> I clung to her and kissed, but senseless as a stone
> Grew that torrid, blissful bosom closely clutched to mine . . .
> Doomed to live alone, in a darksome river-cave
> I dug for my virgin-bride a shallow sandy grave;
> Now day-long, night-long, the river's moaning surge
> Echoes in her deaf ears my bitter, barren dirge.[4]

The development of this story illustrates clearly why primitive
materials are often inherently poetic: the natural is contemplated
in terms of the supernatural, the literal offered in terms of the non-

literal. Obviously it is dangerous for a girl or a woman to cross running water at night or to wander through reeds and rushes beside a stream. Not only is there the risk from water but from snakes and wild animals. All of these perils are focused in the concept of Hili. Slater's use of the situation to present a suicide is unusual because this action is rare among the Bantu. Because of this simple fact, a reader will appreciate the profound distress of the girl who feels that she cannot accept the life to which she has been destined. The rarity becomes the measure of the distress. The author has made good use indeed of his materials.

II   *Natives at Play and Work*

When Slater decided against writing a book in Xhosa and then translating it, he proceeded quite often to observe frankly from the outside. At times his directness takes the form of a comment which is a judgment:

> . . . their wild barbaric music
> Agitates to action the abekweta. . . .[5]

At other times he is descriptive:

> Lately Manzi herded kine,
> Near the Amatola Hills,
> Slaked his thirst on crystal wine
> Bubbling from the mountain rills;
> Sometimes he, with eager lip,
> From stiff udders stole a sip,
> Or, with guilty glance and laugh,
> Snatched a ride upon a calf.

> Manzi—who is hunter keen
> As ever stalked the mountain slope—
> With his greyhound swift and lean
> Chased the nimble antelope,
> Hurled his kerrie with true aim
> At all birds that near him came;
> If a sly snake raised his head,
> Manzi smote, and it was dead! . . . .

> Thus, untutored and untamed,
> Manzi walked the woods and hills
> Careless, naked, unashamed,
> Joyous as the racing rills—
> Laved his limbs in Tyumie's stream,
> Dried them in the sunny beam,
> Rolled upon the grass in play
> Happy as the new-born day.[6]

It will be observed that in the last stanza above the author slips easily into comment and judgment.

Examples of the type given here are extremely simple, but at times Slater passed to writing of a greater density—as in "Clay Cattle." This, too, starts as descriptive and narrative writing, but its ultimate intention is symbolic.

> Riding along towards Hogsback I saw, close by the roadside,
> Laughing and flashing white teeth a sprinkle of Xosa herdboys. . . .
> Naked they squatted and shaped in clay, moist, pliable, yellow,
> Oxen to plough the fields, sinewy, long-horned oxen;
> Big-uddered cows to fill the round-bellied, red calabashes;
> Sturdy, humpbacked bulls, and heifers with silken haunches.
> Naked they sat in the sun, those pigmy gods and creators,
> Moulding from worthless mud the coveted wealth of the Xosa—
> Cattle to dapple the plains and loom like rocks on the hillside,
> Cattle whose sweet soft lowing gladdens the hills in the evening . . .
> Haply, unheeded, their herds had strayed into fields of mealies;
> They would repent at night when an irate father would greet them . . .
> —Laughing they sat in the sun, those light-hearted, heedless herdboys,
> Moulding in dull brown earth their dreams of beckoning beauty.[7]

At the factual level, the author through these clay images identifies much that is important in Xhosa civilization: cattle of the various kinds, milk in the calabashes, and mealies in the fields. Because the actual cattle may have strayed, a part of the realistic surface will be the father's wrath. It is not realism, however, in which the author is interested, though it is his actual setting which begins to establish the direction in which he is moving. When he sees the boys, he is riding toward Hogsback, to him the most beautiful mountain peak in that part of South Africa. His movement in the direction of Hogsback in the Amatola range is taking him through "the deep-grooved vale of the Tyumie." It is upon the plains and hills up from the river and looking toward the mountains that the cattle will "loom like rocks" and whose lowing will "gladden . . . in the evening." Clearly the author is concerned with art and emotion. At the end of the last line the goal is identified in direct language— the boys have had "dreams of beckoning beauty." In "The Karroo," Slater had said of the Bushmen, that their paintings were "signs of their dreams." It is obvious that this attitude does not belong merely to the Xhosas and Bushmen but to Francis Carey Slater.

By now it should be evident that Slater is using the Xhosas as more than mere childhood memories and as more than interesting primitives. Both elements are prominent in the series, but ultimately he seeks to touch those characteristics which are fundamental in human existence: he is beginning to make even the most South African materials a part of world literature.

III   *Lines of Place and Sentiment*

To balance the twenty-five titles in the "Dark Folk" section, Slater offers the same number in the second half of his book. Many of these are brief, often delicate and effective, commemorations of things noticed in the Cape Town environment and places visited at this time. "In Wynberg Park," "On Wynberg Hill," "African Sun," and "Flamingoes at Zeekoe Vlei" resulted from walks around his home. In 1933 Slater and his wife visited Victoria Falls, and from this trip came the motivation for "Zambesi," "Livingstone at the Falls," and "Zambesi Afterglow." Since memories of the Amatola range, especially Hogsback, had entered the "Dark Folk" series, it was natural to find in this collection "Rhymer's Glen: Hogsback," "In the Mist: Hogsback," and "Morning Song: Hogsback." Yet one gathers that the immediate motivation was a visit after long absence.

Most important of the memory pieces in this volume are "The Kloof" and "Scott Centenary." Both are written in elegiacs, which Slater used only when concerned with art and when he wished to transcend the natural. Here he is concerned with art, specifically literature. "The Kloof" was his outdoor reading room when he was a child. Surrounded by natural beauty, he became the discoverer of literary beauty. When he wrote these lines in 1931 (and dedicated them to his wife) he apparently was making a visit to the area. As he views the scenes of his childhood, he begins to think of them in relation to the present and future.

> May I not tread again this uncertain footpath?
>   Dream once more youth's incredible dreams?
> Vexed with the present and awed by the louring future,
>   Peer through the haze of the past?
> That past which now, in the dim enchantment of distance,
>   Glimmers with radiance soft,
> Even as stange roses glow on the eastern skyline
>   When the sun has sunk in the west.[8]

Knowing that this is close to the period in which he had written *Drought*, no reader is surprised to hear Slater saying he is vexed with the present. In childhood he had been guided toward the Kloof by "impatient dreams" along an "inquisitive footpath." Directness is found in the first stanza, but indirection begins to appear in the second stanza. Writing as if descriptively, he identifies with three flowers the environment which enveloped him in his childhood at the Kloof.

> Here the vivid tecoma, unawed by its sober companions
>   Dapples its emerald dress with blossoms fiercer than flame . . .
> Deep in that grove the plumbago puts forth its fairyland flowers,
>   Wefts of luminous mist that stipple the leaf-bidden dusk . . .
> And in that shadowy grove shine the wandering stars of the jasmine,
>   Strips of night's star-freckled sky drifting into the day . . .[9]

Now in the third stanza the author merges the effect of the literature being read by the boy with the three flowers of the Kloof.

> —Oft as I sought my home, in the sombre tints of the twilight,
>   Radiance blossomed around me, music thrilled in the air,
> Radiance blossomed about me, tecoma, plumbago, and jasmine
>   Flowered to strange new beauty of colour, music, and word. . . .[10]

Poetry taught him to notice in new ways the natural world around him, to see "signs and wonders and symbols." Likewise a new human world was revealed to him: "of the sense, as fervent as flaming tecoma," "of the mind, like luminous lovely plumbago," and "of the spirit, like the radiant blooms of the jasmine." Always aware of the stars, Slater now employs a star as his focusing symbol.

The star that merged in its splendour tecoma, plumbago and jasmine,
The star of my morn and eve, star that will comfort my night.[11]

Undoubtedly, to Francis Carey Slater one of the most important efforts of his career was the writing of "The Settlers' Churchyard." Concerning the settlers he has recorded that "The colonization of that vast area known as the Eastern Province was mainly due to them, and they co-operated stoutly in the establishment of Port Elizabeth, East London, Grahamstown, King William's Town, Queenstown and many other towns and villages. The achievements of these British pioneers, their struggles and suffering, their manifold hardships, their patient toil and the innumerable dangers they faced with unfailing fortitude, offer a theme worthy of a great South African epic. I have paid my tribute in an elegy, 'The Settlers' Churchyard.' "[12] In a note on the poem, he has the following to say:

The churchyard referred to in this poem is at Grahamstown, the capital of the Eastern Province. Grahamstown is one of the most beautiful towns in South Africa, and is generally spoken of as the "City of Saints," because of its many churches, or as the "Settlers' City," owing to its connection with the British settlers of 1820. Many of these settlers, together with officers and men who fought in the early Kaffir Wars, are buried in this churchyard. The late Mrs Sampson did much good work towards renovating and beautifying this old cemetery—which had become a wilderness.[13]

Except for the last five stanzas, Slater employs the method of direct historical narrative. He starts as the settlers leave England for South Africa and follows them through the years and to final rest in their graves. There is no attempt to write the story of his own family, though on both sides Slater's great-grandparents were among the 1820 Settlers. The method used is to devote a stanza, usually, to each phase of their movements from old to new and as far as possible describe the new. Thus the narrative starts with a very brief lyric celebration of the England they are leaving and an idealistic hope for homes in this new land of sunshine. Then the scene shifts to the normal three months at sea, the landing "within Algoa's cheerless bay," and the movement inland by ox-wagon.

Differences between the English countryside and South Africa's trackless space shock even the stoutest nervous system. There are strange soils, plants, animals, snakes, and birds. Many of these are deadly. Across the vast area the travelers spread, settle, and begin to

develop the land. Now they discover they must fight pests seeking
to destroy crops and disease to kill off their cattle. Drought is a constant threat. Native raiders fire their ripe fields and drive away their
herds. Yet the settlers endure. A second generation inherits their
attempts, then a third, and with Francis Carey Slater, a fourth. The
land is won for crops, villages grow across the veld, a few cities develop, and a country has come into being. The Settlers of 1820 have
acted out a dream, a dream that they will find a land of sun. They
most certainly find the sun. In fact they often find too much of it.
Yet they learn to live with the South African sun, and writers slowly
come to sense its significance as a symbol. Thus, when Slater reaches
the climax of his story, when the sun has set upon the life of each of
these settlers, he uses the sun as the basis for his summation.

> The sun goes down with golden banners flying,
> The hilltops flame with gestures of farewell,
> He is not dead, though here his beams are dying
> And purple wreaths proclaim his burial;
> He is not dead, but with unfailing might
> He carries on his ceaseless war with night,
> Marshalling on other fields his phalanxes of light. [14]

The setting sun signifying the death of the settlers has in its natural
progress created burial wreaths for them. Though the setting sun
indicates death, the sun itself is not dead. Likewise, the settlers are
no longer physically present; yet the work they started has been continued by their children and grandchildren. They built their homes
in the sun and made the soil around them supply food. They built
churches and schools and hospitals. They helped to push back the
night of centuries which had passed before the settlers came.

Much of Slater's life and heritage is focused in "The Settlers'
Churchyard." His great-grandfather had sought South Africa to
find abundant sunshine. His father, the third generation, was still
living from the soil. Francis himself was born and raised on the farm
and knew all of its work. Xhosa civilization became a part of him before he even knew what was occurring. The same was true of the
language and of all that went with it of the Afrikaans neighbors of
his childhood. Francis was educated at Lovedale beside Xhosa students and until manhood lived in Alice. Twelve banking assign-
ments over more than a quarter of a century had forced him to hold
close to him much of the Eastern Province. Its soil and scenery he

loved. He loved its people, all of them. To him the work of the settlers was worthy of praise for greatness. He touched the subject first
in a major statement in "The Karroo." Then came "The Settlers'
Churchyard." Between these appeared the anonymously published
Drought, showing the profound hurt in one who loved. Then into
the "Dark Folk" volume he introduced "The Rabid Patriot," showing again his distress over the way things were going in South Africa.
Here he has South Africa say,

> Son of my soil, you claim me as your own,
> You slobber over me your love to prove—
> Love that would stay wild seas, high mountains move!
> You bow in awe before my wood and stone,
> You hail my charms in hymns of fervent tone:
> Thus, you maintain your love for me, your mother,
> But how can you love me and hate your brother?[15]

For those who know South Africa, these are not vague general statements. Slater has asked the ultimately relevant question. His own
answer has already been given in *Drought* and in what has been
discussed in this chapter.

IV   *Something Very Special*

Perhaps the easiest of Francis Carey Slater's titles to pass by without proper notice is "The Dead Eagle." In a table of contents the
three words promise very little. A first reading of the lines gives the
impression that here is something very good, one of the author's
best. The danger is that a reader will stop at this point, assuming
that he has examined no more than a well-written piece about a
dead eagle, though, of course, at one level that is what he has read.
Another danger is to assume that the eagle stands only for one particular person or idea and that the eagle is a simple metaphor. What
is wrong with these approaches is that each will make quite simple
a very rich piece of writing.

More at the creating center of the compositional process is the sun
than the image of the eagle. In fact, the first four words identify the
eagle as "Son of the sun." The second stanza speaks of the *sun* as
"The king of eagles—he with eyeball fiery—." Passing from stanza
to stanza, a reader is always aware of the sun. Then, in the final
stanza, the sun, operating at another level, enters the lines.

A golden patch upon the sombre plain
You lie, far from your battlements of granite,
And passers-by pick up a plume and scan it
And hide it in their breasts and pass again:
In days to come those particles of the sun
Within men's solitary hearts will kindle
A steadfast flame, a light that shall not dwindle
When beetles, worms and buzzing flies are gone
To feed the earth they fatten on.[16]

When the king of eagles had first approached and then departed from the young eagle, the king had "sailed away in golden wise." Now when the eagle falls in death, it is shown as "a golden patch upon the sombre plain." The plume which the passersby pick up is identified as "particles of the sun" which "will kindle" in men's hearts "A steadfast flame, a light." Starting with the claim that the eagle is "Son of the sun," the author ends, quite consistently, stating that even in death a feather from the eagle offers "particles of the sun." Before discussing why these particles can kindle a flame, a light, it would be well to return to the beginning lines and make another start, this time a more detailed one.

Worthy of initial attention is the fact that the "Son of the sun" comes into existence at the highest possible point while remaining on earth, among "rugged granite towers" caught in a "fine-spun web of air." Elevation will continue until near the end, where a descent to the plains occurs. The heights would naturally be the place of origin for an eagle. Here, of course, the sun will have easy access to the nest; and the young eagle's first frightening experience is to gaze into the eye of the sun. Yet "snatching heart" he "glories in his gaze." As the sun sped away and darkness approached, fear again seized the young eagle. Soon, however, he found himself gazed upon by countless stars. Thus one great experience follows another. Storms came and beat upon the cliffs. Then from the precipices the young eagle looked down into shadowy depths. Continued awareness of the sun exists in such lines as the following, where in abysses

. . . sluggard shadows unmolested sleep
Till roused at noon they turn and sleep once more. . . .[17]

Evidence that the author is writing about men and not eagles and

that he has at least one man in mind as his symbol appears in the fifth stanza and becomes even more complete in the sixth. As the eyes of the young eagle rake the distance, he gazes over the plains and sees shadows there. Then of him is asked, at that time "did not the coiled campaign/Stir in your infant brain?"[18] Yet for a while he remained among his granite towers, "Companioned by the sunlight and the stars," where "The human storm . . . came not near [him]."[19] Finally, after what suggests a period of preparation, the young eagle leaves his mountain home for the plains.

> Then springing from your mountain-towers you flew
> Over their fretted spires in triumph screaming,
> And reaped the heavens with your great scythes gleaming,
> Binding with golden swathes their sheaves of blue;
> And swooping down, in wider circles sweeping,
> You saw the riddle of the plains unroll
> In amplitudinous and crinkled scroll
> Dotted with towns, like mushroom clusters peeping,
> Where ant-like men were creeping.[20]

Immediately the death-lines appear.

> Son of the sun, death's unseen shaft has found you,
> And endless night—dark is your matchless vision!
> Your wings that held the tempest in derision
> Are stiller than the grass which whispers round you. . . .[21]

Now that which was physical is devoured by the earth's scavengers. The feathers, normally what would be left, become symbolic of the influence which passes beyond earth.

Indication that Slater at this time associated eagle and man comes from the fact that a year before writing "The Dead Eagle" he had written a poem to Roy Campbell, then in his middle twenties, in which he had addressed him as the Young Eagle, "Soar Again, Young Eagle." There is no question of whether or not Roy Campbell is the person intended in the later poem. Because of the epigraph, the initial candidate would have to be Shelley, for whom Slater had great admiration and who was much given to soaring through upper space. Yet a reader hesitates to restrict the nominations to Shelley. General Smuts, highly respected by Slater and a great admirer of Shelley, would fit well into the poem, though he still had many years to live. Raising the question of politics should draw forth at least one such nomination, especially since at this moment Slater was deeply involved in such thinking and had exploded in *Drought* and "The Rabid Patriot." Yet the best approach is to suggest the presence of universal characteristics in the lines, especially the viewing of the world and man's affairs with poetic sight.

Immediately before the descent to the plains, the entry into the world, the preparation stanza stresses contact with a vast natural environment.

> Companioned by the sunlight and the stars,
> You knew not apathy nor sterile langour;
> The human storm, the iterated clangour
> And tumult of men's never-ceasing wars,
> With sullen reverberations came not near you:
> In desert silence, shoreless solitude,
> You bartered youth among your mountains rude,
> The brimming beaker of the dawn to cheer you,
> And heaven stooping near you:[22]

Silence, solitude, space belong to no man but to all men. Sun and stars look down upon mankind, and each man may look back to them in the heavens. In the universe there is no war, but eternal harmony. Man makes war across his earthly plains, bringing death with its "endless night." Yet beyond the darkness which comes to one generation is the light which can exist for the next, as the "particles of the sun" bring *flame, light*—another day. Both "flame" and "light" offer implications of love and truth. Thus, though there is another day which in the physical sense follows the night, there is that which transcends the material world.

In "The Dead Eagle," which he placed at the end of *Dark Folk and Other Poems*, Francis Carey Slater achieved something which he was never to surpass, though his most ambitious work was yet to be written. After a life of devotion to his country, he had come to transmute her most particular and typical substance into the symbolic. "The Karroo" had employed the soil and climate; *Dark Folk* utilized the native element; *The Trek* was to study the Dutch in South Africa. He himself as he wrote was a constant reminder of what the English had done and were still doing. Along with much else, they had endured.

CHAPTER 14

Afrikaans History, The Trek, *1938*

A CTIONS of the kind present in what South African history calls the Great Trek always present material which will engage the imagination. The initial appeal is to the principal events as adventure, ignoring almost completely the fact that decisions which guide human lives are involved. Of course the Great Trek was in every way a magnificent adventure, confronting those who undertook it with much of the opposition the world has to offer. The men who planned the migration had to arrange the movement of large numbers of men, women, and children—together with great herds and all household and farm equipment. Everything except the herds had to be taken by ox-drawn vehicles across country without roads. Food for both man and beast had to be found along the way. All of this was done while moving first across a desert area and always against uncertain weather conditions. There were wild animals to guard against and primitive tribes in every direction. The inevitable result was going to be war—before the end, finally, total war between trekkers and Zulus.

Born a full generation after the events, Slater as a boy must have known the happenings from story and legend. As a youth and young banker he lived where many of the trekkers started, but the territory to which they went was beyond his direct experience. Xhosas he knew, but the Zulus existed in the world of his imagination. As he grew older, much of this material must in his mind have assumed its place as history. Finally, when at the age of sixty he came to write *The Trek*, his purpose was rather complicated.

According to the author, he had long contemplated writing on the subject. Starting his work more than two full years before the centenary celebration of the Great Trek, he gave himself time to make a careful study of the materials concerned with the history of the Voortrekkers. Both study and writing were completed in time for the volume to appear during the centenary period, December,

1938. Though Slater says the book was written for his Afrikaner fellow countrymen, they ignored or rejected his work. Very soon a reader understands why repudiation occurred: as author, he did not stop with presentation of the strength of the trekkers, especially the leaders, but also developed their very human weaknesses.

I   *More Than a Story*

If a reader does not already know South African history, he will be surprised to discover that the Great Trek was not one vast movement but a number of individual groups starting from various points, at different times, under separate leaders. Not even their destinations were the same. Final settlement found them not only miles but provinces apart. Thus, though there is much action, a single narrative is impossible, except on the basis of selection of some small part of the total movement. Because Slater was working with a manifold purpose, his surface structure is very loose.

Using a prelude and an epilogue as a frame and thirty interspersed lyrics for relief, emphasis, and comment, the author destroys at once any expectation of a narrative approach. Furthermore, the body of the work is in rhyming couplets, certainly not a narrative instrument. Then, too, he makes more than one start. Gerrit Maritz and his party left from Graaff-Reinet in August, 1836; Louis Trigardt and his group moved out from the valley of the Indwe River in May, 1835; Hendrik Potgieter and his trekkers departed from Tarka in February, 1836; Sarel Cilliers and his thirty wagons made up of Liebenbergs, Britses, Broekhuisers, van Rensbergs, and Krugers left Colesberg and joined with the trek of Hendrik Potgieter; Piet Retief set out from the Winterberg in 1837 and gathered wagons as he moved, until at the Orange River he had a hundred tented wagons and a hundred and twenty armed men; Piet Uys left from Uitenhage in April 1837. This is the order in which the various treks are introduced; and before Piet Uys is mentioned, the great engagement at Vegkop had been fought, where forty trekkers had defeated five thousand Matabele warriors, and also the raid upon Umsilikazi's kraals had been made, and Louis Trigardt had reached his Promised Land. Thus, as a ball of string, the whole grows larger and more entangled as the months pass.

Because of the way in which he has introduced the individual leaders, it is evident that Slater is interested in the fundamental nature of the men who created the history with which he is working. It is assumed that these men have something in common since they were willing to abandon an established home and accept hardship as they sought a new, unknown land. Not merely because Slater was interested in it, but that which made these men characters who created history is the fact that each was unique and each believed in himself. These qualities were not always an advantage; yet life with such men is never dull. Wherever they might go, action was to accompany them.

Each of the men in charge of a group had been placed in his position of leadership because he was respected and trusted by those who knew him best. These commanders were men of experience and ambition, of devotion and strength, of courage and persistence. They were not, however, indoctrinating their followers with new ideas. Both leaders and followers were very much alike in their thinking, though it is doubtful that either was totally aware of the source of an urge to trek. One of the often avowed reasons was the desire to get away from towns and government, governments which in Slater's phrase imposed "tactless laws." Thus men longed to leave behind the oppressiveness of organized society and to be free. The desire for freedom is, of course, not new. What changes from land to land and from age to age is the context in which that desire operates.

Presentation of the South African context gave Slater his chance. Here living in the nineteenth century was a group looking upon itself as the chosen people starting out to find the Promised Land. The Old Testament was going to be lived again in the modern world. The first trek Slater presents is that of Gerrit Maritz, which leaves from Graaff-Reinet, "that dappled gem/ On the desert's dusty hem." Despite the desirable qualities of Graaff-Reinet, the trekkers are "Lured by the beckoning beauty of Far-Away" and start out across the burning Karroo. On their first Sunday, Father Smit delivers a sermon on how

> The tribes of Israel trekked from Egypt's Land
> Thro' the Red Sea and toiled across the sand
> Of foodless wastes, where they from heaven were fed;
> How thro' each day those wanderers were led
> By cloud-built pillars; and how each night a flame
> Of fire beckoned them until they came
> At last to the Promised Land of their desire.[1]

On and on Maritz in his sky-blue wagon leads his group until they
cross the "Orange River, whose red-brown flood . . . curled thro'
tawny veld towards the sea."[2]

> Onward the trekkers trailed thro' a new "free state,"
> Onward with burgeoning hopes and . . .
> On, toward the appointed meeting-place,
> At Blesberg highlands . . .
> Maritz, with his way-worn cattle and weary men
> Settled, and rested from their long travel-toil
> In quietude upon a friendly soil.
> And here they welcomed, as the days went by,
> Small treks that dribbled in from far and nigh
> To join their ranks beneath a new "free" sky.[3]

This area became known finally as the Orange Free State. Thus, in
his first section, Slater has developed the idea of searching for a
land in which they could be free.

Appearing second but actually more than a year earlier in time
is the trek led by Louis Trigardt. This group likewise crossed the
Orange River but moved on north by northeast across the Caledon
and finally the Vaal.

> But ever on and on, North and North-East,
> Stout Trigardt pressed with weary man and beast,
> Till far beyond the Vaal he came at last
> To pleasant highlands, breezy and well-grassed,
> Foothills of rugged mountains . . .
>   Here in these highlands Trigardt made a stand,
> Ended his first long trek; and now his band
> Built little houses and rough gardens planned
> With dams and water-furrows all complete.
> In this remote Arcadian retreat
> Trigardt and all his followers will stay . . .

In the Transvaal, beyond Johannesburg and Pretoria, lies the town
which perpetuates the memory of Louis Trigardt. His group had
traveled the greatest distance from the old towns of the Cape. If
to get away from towns and governments was to be free, Trigardt
had brought his followers to that land which would give the most
freedom. In this remote region they could expect peace.

Next to be described is the trek of Hendrick Potgieter, who after he crossed the Orange was joined by Sarel Cilliers. Together they journeyed on past friendly Griquas and later Smiling Basutos.

> Then sailed the trekkers thro' an emerald sea
> Of undulating grass that, noiselessly,
> Hurled its broad billows, rolling unconfined,
> League upon league some tall blue beach to find.[5]

> And when mild May was running into June
> They came upon a stream which seemed to swoon
> Among its sands: this as the River Sand
> Was known thereafter. In the grass-glad land,
> Around this sand-choked stream, the trekker-band
> Made a long outspan after weary toil,
> And rested three-score days upon "free soil."[6]

Always restless, Potgieter, probably the best fighter of them all, after extensive explorations, joined forces with Maritz at Blesberg.

Starting with this first mass union, it is obvious that the idea of a united trekker organization is beginning to grow. Soon the first "leader-to-be" is introduced, Piet Retief. It is granted Retief to see the Promised Land but not to possess it. Retief was to give his life in an effort to secure Natal for the trekkers. Pretorius is to lead them on to victory, but as yet he has not been mentioned, nor has Retief yet looked out upon the land that beckons him to claim it. Discouraged by the very real problems of leadership and defeated in his effort to bring under one command the different groups, Retief with only some twenty wagons left around him had pushed on into the rugged peaks of the Drakensberg, dividing the highveld from the land which rolled on to the sea.

> . . . awed, he tarried, breathless and amazed
> At the power and glory circling round him there:
> Flashes of Heaven, visions following prayer! . . .
>   Gazing afar from his high pedestal,
> He saw the radiant region of Natal
> Sweeping away, a ruffled sea of green
> And rounded hills, dappled with groves serene
> Of shining trees . . .
>   And in that vast and tingling solitude,
> "In silence in the visionary mood,"
> He mused and meditated late and long—

This poet, unawares, whose only song
Was action, action. . . .
    And as he stood and gazed with eager eyes on
The radiant Land that rolled to the horizon,
Dipping beyond that to an unseen ocean,
His restless soul was stirred to strange emotion,
His being quickened with a "sense sublime,"
That soared beyond the reach of prose or rhyme;
A sense of dedication, of high power
To meet the claims of each exacting hour;
He felt that he, none other, was the Moses
Who . . . would lead the trekker-band:
And while he mused and watched, the Promised Land
Summoned with silent voice, beckoned with unseen hand.[7]

With fifteen men, Retief explored the land and sent back a report.

As those twelve spies, by Moses sent, returned
With clustered grapes—those glowing grapes that shook
Their globes of sunlight over Eschol's brook. . . .
So, to the waiting camp, at last there came
Retief's two riders bearing tropic fruits. . . .
    The messengers in haste
Gave, with their offerings ambrosial,
Glad tidings of Retief's great ride as well
And his successful quest. The camp went wild. . . .[8]

Here ends dreaming, vision. All else will be action, hardship, fight-
ing, and death—until finally victory comes at Blood River. Vision
had been part of the motivation which started the wagons, which
moved them across the desert, rivers, and mountains. But there is
more in the story than vision.

    There was war, war which ended with the destruction of the
Zulus. But war did not come suddenly, and it did not involve all of
the native tribes. Maritz received kindness from Moroka, chief of
the Baralongs. Even before he left the Indwe River, Trigardt had
lived in peace with the Xhosa tribes, and he passed all of the distance to the Zoutpansberg without trouble. Potgieter and Cilliers
found the Griquas friendly and the Basutos, under their great chieftain Moshesh. Trouble came from the Matabeles, whose chief was
Umsilikazi, formerly one of Chaka's captains. Chaka was usually
considered the most skillful and terrible of all Zulu battle leaders

and the Zulus as the most warlike of all Bantu tribes. In retaliation for death, capture, and looting by the Matabeles, Potgieter built a wagon fort and with forty trekkers defeated five thousand Matabeles. Then Potgieter organized a counterraid and captured over seven thousand cattle. This, of course, was the beginning, not the end.

As the trekkers moved into Natal, they understood that it was necessary to deal with Dingaan, king of Zululand. Speaking for the trekkers, Retief wrote to Dingaan and with a party of five was received at the capital, Umgungundhlovu. Retief was promised that his request for land would be granted, but that first he must retrieve and return cattle stolen from Dingaan by a petty chief, Sikonyela. The cattle were returned, but many who knew Dingaan well began to warn Retief against dealing with him and especially against visiting his capital. Many of the trekker leaders became alarmed and begged Retief not to risk his life, but Retief insisted and set out with seventy men and thirty grooms. On February 3, 1838, they were formally received, and three days later Dingaan signed a deed giving to the Trekker company the lands from the Tugela River south to the Umzimvubu. Now the king proposed a final celebration in his central kraal, all to come without arms as a sign of friendship. By this time company after company of the king's warriors had entered the kraal. Their dances became the entertainment. Finally, the "black dancing wave, fringed with the bright/ Sharp foam of spears, curled in its gathering might/ And shook its crest."[9] Dingaan gave the signal, and the ring became the "inner circle of Hell." No man in Retief's party was ever seen again.

Now Dingaan sent out his regiments to dispose of all the trekkers in the whole area.

> On a wide front and in a murky night,
> The Zulu impis opened up the fight.
> Upon the scattered wagon-camps they crept,
> And slaughtered many trekker-folk, who slept
> In tranquil ease unconscious of all ill.[10]

> Five hundred folk were slain in that black night;
> Many bore wounds; all were in woeful plight;
> And that sad region sown with rich red grain
> As Weenen—"place of weeping," place of pain—
> Was known thenceforth.[11]

Completely dismayed at first, groups soon began to assemble, organize, and consider ways of opposing Dingaan. Potgieter and Piet Uys brought help. Again, the Zulus lured the trekker forces into a trap. Piet Uys was killed, and his fourteen-year-old son died defending his father. Torrential rains fell; fever and measles spread; foot-and-mouth disease was rife among the cattle. The Zulus struck at a settlement separated from the main group under Maritz. Suddenly Maritz died.

Having reached what now appeared to be the lowest possible level in their hopes, the trekkers began to receive help. Friends in Cape Town had sent a ship to Port Natal with supplies of all kinds. From Graaff-Reinet, Andries Pretorius set out with reinforcements. He sent word that the trekkers were to prepare to fight the Zulu king. At once the camps began to work toward a major engagement with Dingaan's forces. On November 22, Pretorius with his men reached the Headquarters camp, and he was made commandant of the Company of Trekkers. Final preparations were completed, and on November 28 a force of five hundred men crossed the Tugela and pushed toward Umgungundhlovu. From time to time there were skirmishes, but Pretorius guarded against the type of trap into which Piet Uys had ridden. On Saturday, December 15, they made camp beside a river, expecting to keep the Sabbath there, but they took no chances. On one side the river gave protection and on the other a deep ravine. Carefully they fortified the open sides.

> . . . The wagons almost tilt to tilt
> Were drawn and lashed with trek-chains end to end;
> Raw hides were then stretched tightly to defend
> The outer wheels, while under and between
> The wagons heavy stones and thorn-trees green
> Were tightly packed. Against the wagon-screen
> Ladders were placed for fighting men to use.[12]

When night fell, all was finished. The battle preparations proved to have been quite wise, for the Sabbath was not to be kept in worship.

> When the sun lit the lamps of myraid dews
> Upon December's fateful sixteenth day,
> The Boers were braced and ready for the fray.

Gazing around, they saw "all Zululand"
March to the attack, a multitudinous band—
Countless as locusts—all in war array.
Shouting and drumming on their shields they came,
Dark wave on wave fringed with the foam of spears;
And as they came the Boers with joyous cheers
Met the black tide with waves of smoke and flame
From thundering muskets.
    Upon a day so bright,
"As if ordained," each Boer could mark the sight
Of his snaphaan. Powder was plentiful
And slugs also—a handful of each one
Rammed hurriedly into each smoking gun,
And then the trekker marksmen point and pull
And swift death follows.
    All around a sea
Of sable forms rolled on amid the smoke.
On and yet on it swept, but finally
It paused in hesitation and then broke
In a great backward wave. Then, like a trumpet, spoke
Pretorius and bade the burghers charge
Upon the foe, who wavered and then fled
Hotly pursued. Upon the broken marge
Of the swift river countless warriors bled
Hiding beneath their shields; while many a score
Floating like otters—noses above the kind
Brim of the river—soon incarnadined
Its crystal surface with their crimson gore.
Thereafter that clear stream, whose waters quiver
Beneath each breeze, was known as the Blood River;
And as Blood River Battle was the fight
Known, that took place beside its waters bright.[13]

Here was the perfect dramatic conclusion for a story of action, and except for the epilogue this is where Slater ended. Yet to create the account given above, it has been necessary to select from a mass of additional material. *The Trek* as a whole does not present this type of organization.

II *The Destroying Divisiveness*

Nothing given so far offers the point of final significance in this important piece of South African history. The conflict which is most in need of examination is not that between Boer and Zulu but that within the Boers themselves, between creative and destructive qualities existing within one man and ultimately one people. In truth, this is the story of mankind, which gives *The Trek* its universal quality; yet Slater has localized and individualized the narrative to give it South African relevance.

Certainly the supreme example of the constructive and destructive principle operating within the same man should be, and is, the leader of the trekkers, Piet Retief. Long before the beginning of the Great Trek, Retief had demonstrated his ability to succeed in the practical world, whether in the city or upon the land. He was also obviously a leader of men, both in war and in peace. His actions showed him to be an unselfish man concerned for the welfare of others. When at fifty-seven he assumed command of the Trek, no one of the other possible leaders was his equal in experience and in what he had done for his fellow man. As commander he made every effort to create harmony among the various factions of the Trek. The rules which he made for daily life among the people were wise, and his orders with military significance concerning conduct and movement were, as events proved, the correct ones. All of his practical abilities were controlled by vision, something of the spirit. Here, the trekkers thought, was the one who could guide them to the Promised Land. Yet within Retief there was weakness, for unto no man is everything given. In handling Retief's dealings with Dingaan, Slater shows very clearly the deficiencies which led to destruction. After the first interview with the Zulu king, Retief on the return trip visited an American missionary, Pastor Champion, who knew well the ways of Dingaan. Firmly the missionary warned Retief not to approach the king with a commando.

> Superior, Retief lightly replied,
> That "Kaffir ways" were well within his ken,
> That Afrikanders and not Englishmen
> "Understood Kaffirs." Champion stressed his doubt:
> Different were eastward tribes, he pointed out,
> From fierce war-welded fighting Zulu folk.
> And then, with pride, he added quietly
> That a true born American was he.
> Retief replied, laughing at his own joke,
> That the good Missionary, Champion,
> Tho' born and bred a true "American,"

> Was just as near being an "Englishman"
> "As made no difference" betwixt one and one.[14]

Here the weakness displayed in none other than the first of the Seven Deadly Sins—pride. Assumption of Afrikaans superiority inevitably led to viewing with scorn the English and Americans.

Another extremely human trait displayed by Retief was his failure to notice the nature and implications of his own words and actions, something that he would have seen immediately in another. Slater shows this weakness in discussing his most important message of several sent to Dingaan.

> Further he stressed, with gusto, the severe
> Defeat of Umsilikazi at the hands
> Of Maritz and Potgieter's chastening bands.
> Lastly, he said, the predikants would show,
> From Holy Writ, the agony and woe . . .
> That God had wreaked of old on wicked kings:
> A subtle hint that Umsilikazi soon
> Might be invisible to sun and moon.
> —Great Homer nods, sometimes, just as a thistle
> Bobs to the breeze: even so, in this epistle,
> The writer nodded, or was transiently insane.[15]

Nothing is more characteristic of man than to become guilty of the very thing most abhorred in one's enemy. Dingaan's deceit is the quality blamed in viewing events of this period. Yet in retrieving Dingaan's cattle, Retief resorted to a similar deceit.

> By means of friendly word
> Sent by Retief the robber-chief was lured
> To the commando-camp, and there endured
> Captivity until he should restore
> The Zulu king's three hundred head of kine,
> Together with four hundred cattle more
> As bail for future conduct, or as fine
> For past misdeeds. His guns and horses, too,
> His captors took. . . .[16]

As Retief turned from dealing with those who were not his own, he displayed the very essence of pride. At the moment when he most needed to listen to the advice of his associates, he heard only himself.

. . . Leaders met
In council: Gert Maritz and eloquent
Cilliers, and others. By fresh fears beset,
All were uneasy now; and one and all
Besought their friend and governor not to go
In person to the Zulu monarch's kraal.
   Gerrit Maritz . . . offered to go instead,
Since *his* death "would not mean so much," he said
As his great chief's. But the latter gave no heed
To warnings; he was leader and must lead. . . .[17]

From his own Bible, Retief should have learned how important it
was to accept counsel. Yet he heeded no one and rode swiftly to his
death—carrying with him many others.

Often the conflict within a human being or between one man
and another grows from the difference between theory and practice. Few men enunciate evil principles; yet what men do often
bears little resemblance to their announced purposes. All of the
trekkers agreed that the aim of the Great Trek was to discover the
Promised Land. Their intentions were clear; but as soon as they
began to practice them, there was confusion.

One bristling question teased the Trekker-band,
Day in, day out, where lay the Promised Land?
Was it the High Veld, or was it the Low?
Was it to North? Or East thro' mountain-snow?
Where lay the Canaan to which all should go?

   Potgieter voted North, for he had seen
Beyond the Vaal the grasslands waving green,
Barred with the silver of vivacious springs
And starred with flowers, a Land for cattle-kings.
Further he stressed the point, political,
That the enticing region of Natal,
Basking in beauty by the passionate sea,
An easy prey to England's ships might be,
Not so the inland North.

               But Piet Retief . . .
Favoured Natal . . .
Eastward he now moved slowly; after him
Waveringly came Maritz . . .

Whilst, hesitant and tardy, far behind
Gaunt Potgieter, his stubborn thoughts inclined
To the magnetic North . . .
And in the valley of the Caledon,
Far to the South, dauntless Piet Uys began
To take the rearguard with his waiting clan.[18]

Retief at Tafelkop—to test his strength—
Held a great trekker-gathering; and there
Was wrangling, argument and blaze and blare
Between the "Opposition" and the "Government."
Muskets were flourished; gossamer-silence rent
By angry sharp-toned voices; and at last
Piet Uys flung out; and, as he hurried past,
"Where are we going?" someone asked, "please say!"
And Uys said, "Each is going his own way,
One forward and the next aside but none
Following!"[19]

Again and again conflict erupted as the treks moved on. The first
individual conflict came between Trigardt and van Rensburg. This
trek was the earliest of all, starting in May, 1835. In presenting
this first disagreement, Slater foreshadows what is to follow.

Right ready fighters were the trekker-men,
Prone to dissension, quick in quarrel, and when
No foes were near they clashed one with another—
Father with son, or brother against brother.
"Lange Hans" van Rensburg to this rule was not
A meek exception: so after quarrel hot
His trek and Trigardt's parted, even as Lot
And Abraham parted in the days of yore.
Hans and his trek turned East, and nevermore
Were seen of white-skinned men.[20]

Of the trekkers in general, the author remarks, "These Boers, great
pioneers in their great day,/ Were dour, suspicious, impatient of all
sway/ Even by their chosen leaders."[21] Again, he says of them,

. . . Therefore did they maintain,
Fiercely, the fight, in which no foes are slain,
The war of politics, the bliss and bane
Of Afrikaner-folk—who, to this day,

> Quarrel and wrangle in the same sad way.[22]

It was not until Retief, Maritz, Uys—and unnamed hundreds with them—were dead that Pretorius for a brief period had enough unity to achieve victory at Blood River.

Very early Slater comments upon the amazing proneness towards dissension, even in religious matters.

> Grievous it is, incredible and odd,
> How good folk quarrel in the name of God:
> To many Christians their specific creed
> Means more than Christ and more than Christ-like deed.[23]

Throughtout the trek there was argument over the position to be taken by various predikants or pastors. So often was Father Smit the cause of trouble that the author surmised he should be compared with Helen herself in creating strife.

In the epilogue the author asks the question,

> Their strength's beyond us, but their weaknesses
> We equal or excel with fatal ease,
> For do we not, my brothers, to this day,
> Wrangle and quarrel in the old sad way?[24]

If Slater expected Afrikaans readers to admire his work, he was having the same difficulty displayed by Retief in his letter to Dingaan.

III *Symbolically*

Often in his writing Slater makes use of vision, both the word and the idea. Section IV of his Prelude to *The Trek* is called "Vision." A reader assumes that this is the vision which drew the trekkers on their way. Soon he learns, however, that the vision was Slater's, and what he saw was an imagined movement of these great figures of South African history. The author, then, is proceeding from a literary rather than from a historical point of view. He feels as well as thinks his subject. Strong emphasis is given to this attitude by the lyrics interspersed throughout the whole. Some of these have little to do with the Trek but much to do with South Africa. The travelers naturally saw hundreds of springboks, but this beautiful small buck had no peculiar association with the trek-

kers. Millions know the springbok, however, as an emblem of South
Africa. Slater has also added to his "Karroo Collection" with verses
such as "Groves of Stone" and "No Marble Marks the Memory."
The story of the battle at Vegkop is given as a lyric rather than in
the narrative portion of the work. Finally, Slater concludes with a
lyric of praise using some of the materials which mean South Africa
to him.

> The grim Karroo is ours:
>   Whose barren sunburnt plains
> Melt suddenly into a mist of flowers
>   After long-waited rains:
>
> Whose hoarded glories unclose,
>   At dawn and day's decline,
> When sombre koppies are isles of rose
>   In seas of amber wine.
>
> Our Dragon Peaks that rise
>   —Vast billows foamed with cloud—
> Surge magnificently to the sky's
>   Shores serene and proud. . . .
>
> Here amid infinite space
>   May mind and spirit expand,
> Making us worthy of time and a place
>   In this our Sunshine Land.
>
> Her silence sings to the soul:
>   She beckons with unseen hand
> Where surly seas bellow and roll
>   'Twixt us and her bright strand.
>
> Unto this earth we own,
>   Love, and serve while we live,
> Our blood and bone for fountain and stone
>   After life shall we give.[25]

Though there is no evidence that Slater had any preconceived
plan to encompass all of South Africa in what he wrote, with the
completion of *The Trek* it was clear that he was actually coming very
close to fulfilling such a purpose. With the arrival of full maturity,

he obviously was beginning to employ earth and climate symbolically. To his Englishness he had assimilated both the Dark Folk and the Dutch—all beneath the South African sun. Few people seem to realize not only that there is sun in the Karroo and the Kalahari but that vast areas of South Africa have some two hundred days of sun essentially unbroken through the winter. The highveld can in many ways boast one of the finest climates in the world, in both summer and winter. Thus the sun as fact can with justice become a symbol. Under this shining symbol Slater has accepted the Afrikaans people whether or not they have accepted him.

CHAPTER 15

The Gathering: Editor, 1945;
Selected Poems, 1947; Veld Patriarch,
1949; Collected Poems, 1957

I Editor

BETWEEN 1939 and 1944, Slater suffered several severe illnesses, resulting from duodenal ulcers, which at times caused internal hemorrhages. In 1944, at sixty-eight, he underwent major surgery, from which he emerged with improved health. Immediately he began a complete revision of the *Centenary Book of South African Verse*, 1925. The early collection had sold well not only in South Africa but also in England, but between 1925 and 1945 what had been written was destined to replace much composed during the first hundred years. In the mid-1920's, young men who would achieve world recognition began to publish. Among these were Roy Campbell and William Plomer. This shift of balance is shown by observing that in the 1945 volume the first author who is still living appears on page forty-seven of a two-hundred-and-eighteen-page chronologically arranged anthology.

In every possible way, the new collection is an improvement upon the first book, as the 1925 edition showed development beyond all that had preceded the Slater gathering. One extremely important manifestion of what was happening is demonstrated by the prescribing of the *New Centenary Book* for the University Senior Certificate Examination and also for the University Matriculation Examination. What had been on trial, of course, was not Slater but South African writing. University recognition was evidence of the achievement to be found, and time has supported the opinion of the universities.

With few exceptions, the work of these younger writers dealt with South African materials, as had that of their fathers and grand-fathers. What changed was the way in which the material was being used. Description was absorbed into action and grew dramatic. Objects were turned into symbols and began to impinge upon the reader on more than one level. South African details assumed universal aspects. Local substance was still present in abundance; mere local color had disappeared. South African literature was becoming a world literature, and Francis Carey Slater was doing much to help with the process of giving his country first to his country and finally to the world.

II   *Selected Poems*

When he had finished the new anthology of South African verse, the seventy-year-old lover of South Africa and of poetry gave his attention to revising and preparing for the press his own formerly published work, which now dated back more than forty years. He sent the completed typescript to his friend R. C. K. Ensor, historian and poet, whom he had last visited at Corpus Cristi, Oxford, in 1938. It was upon this occasion that he had met Edmund Blunden, now to become important in the publication of Slater's intended collection of his own work.

Upon receiving the typescript, Ensor conferred with the Oxford University Press and obtained their promise to publish a selected but not a collected edition. The press suggested Edmund Blunden as the person to make the choice of material to be used. Slater accepted the Oxford offer, provided the whole of *Drought* was included. At the request of the publisher, Ensor contributed a short biographical introduction. All involved in the plan agreed, and the printing of the book proceeded. In May, 1947, *Selected Poems* appeared. It contained *Drought* in its entirety and the whole of "The Karroo." There were twenty-four of the pieces from the "Dark Folk" collection. Fifteen lyrics were chosen and five narrative-historical-elegiac selections; also fifteen items from *The Trek* and its epilogue. Two war titles were added. Slater estimated that this was about two-thirds of what he wished to retain of all the verse he had written.

In the introduction, Ensor is very firm when suggesting that any-one who is almost completely self-taught will develop slowly. Between 1905 and 1919 Slater had published four volumes of verse, but he finally considered almost all of this as apprentice work. Both Slater and Ensor believed the permanent work started with "The Karroo," 1924. This is the obvious reason for wishing its inclusion, though seemingly Blunden did not concur. The publisher added to the book a note which explains that "The Karroo" is "included at the insistence of another [than Blunden]." Whether it was the author, Ensor, or someone else who insisted upon this inclusion is not very important. It seems rather certain that both Slater and his English supporter believed that the very best work began with *Drought* and continued through the next two volumes. This means that Slater's final reputation rests upon writing done between the ages of fifty-two and sixty-two, 1928-38.

In his introduction and in letters to the author, Ensor praises Francis Carey Slater in the expected ways. Yet the most important evidence of his feelings will be found in a statement which he never expected to be seen by more than one person. For Christmas, 1938, he sent a copy of *The Trek* to Frank Nutt. There is also extant a letter to Nutt of the kind normal between friends. One paragraph of this communication offers a very important observation.

> I ventured to send you myself F. C. Slater's *The Trek*; a poem that you might easily have overlooked, since the [?] who control poetry reviewing seem so far to have successfully deprived it of all reviews in this country. I think it very good poetry in parts (not all parts), and also very taking as a sort of national epic—the glorification of a country and nation by a poet body-and-soul devoted to them. When you know how the Malecrites have striven to make The Trek an anti-English symbol, then the fact that the Trek's finest celebration is in English (for I am told on good authority that none of the Dutch writers have done anything so large) becomes very remarkable. It was only possible because S. is a singularly large-hearted man who loves his country in the most comprehensive way.[1]

Why Ensor was ready to help Slater is clearly revealed by this letter. There were, of course, two reasons for the new edition. It would get into print material which was no longer available, and even a selection would be the beginning of a final focusing. At last the process was starting. Yet Slater was far from satisfied with what was to him a partial book.

III   *Veld Patriarch*

Immediately after *Selected Poems* was issued, the author took the

material rejected by Edmund Blunden (added slightly to it) and sub-
mitted it to another publisher, who brought this out under the title
Veld Patriarch and Other Poems, 1949. The volume of selections
made by Blunden had totaled a hundred and eighty pages; the
"remainder" was only seventy-seven pages. One can see very easily
why the author had wished to have everything in one book as a final
collection. The movement of man's affairs, however, is strange;
and when the conclusion of this author's career is reached, it is quite
possible to feel that he had benefited from the separate publications.

Apparently not even Slater had expected a collected edition to
carry the whole of *The Trek*, which in the first edition had run to a
hundred and fifty-six pages. What Edmund Blunden had chosen
was a group of the interspersed lyrics, which could in isolation more
easily than any other material in *The Trek* retain whatever power
was originally present in the total context. The author, however,
was unable to forget his characters, the important people of his
story, and thus in the new collection he selected twenty-nine additional "bits and pieces," portraits of the leaders, descriptions of terrain, developments of atmosphere, and some of the main incidents.
All of this totals only twenty-six pages. The weakness of both approaches to *The Trek* is obvious: much of the impact derives from
relationships and juxtapositions. *The Trek* can only be judged when
both people and events are present. Later the author's spirit was to
be at rest. In 1957, before his death, a true collected edition was
published. Here for the future is reproduced, along with all of his
other major work, the full text of his last important literary effort.

Meanwhile, *Veld Patriarch* had its own particular contribution to
make in the development of Slater's reputation. A small individual
volume could give emphasis in several ways which might not be
available in a book offering everything. The author immediately
grasped the opportunity to reprint the title piece, "Veld Patriarch,"
written in 1909, forty years into the past. Two aspects of these five
pages were of personal significance to Slater. The lines of the first
half present Oom Piet, the veld patriarch, representing the Afrikaans neighbors of childhood and the farmers of his banking days—
the Dutch part of the South African population, of whom he had
vast knowledge and for whom he had great love. In reaction to the
land, the soil itself, Oom Piet looks forward to certain aspects of
"The Karroo," 1924, and *Drought*, 1929. That Oom Piet merges
with the particular qualities of South African soil and sun is enough

to account for the retention of his story. In addition, the old man is presented with one of Slater's favorite scenes viewed from the stoep of his white-walled farmhouse.

> Before us, billowing against the sky,
> The Dragon Mountains heaved their giant heads—
> Storm-scarred and battered, blackened by the sun
> And corrugated by the inveterate wind.[2]

Near the end of 1901, Slater had been sent by the bank to Matatiele, in East Griqualand, and here for the first time saw the Drakensberg. An early morning view of the town upon his first day was quite depressing until he raised his eyes to what he in his autobiography called "the gigantic blue-barrier of the Drakensberg. . . . Here was ample compensation for the drab appearance of the village; here was eternal beauty to solace one in sorrow or depression, and solemn grandeur to quicken and inspire the spirit with the joy of elevated thought."[3] Though expressed in the words of William Wordsworth, there is no reason to doubt the actuality of the feeling. What he saw in 1901 seems to have made an impression which remained vivid for fifty years, when he wrote the passage given above.

Regardless of the very real importance of all said about Oom Piet and the land and the mountains, there was something else in "Veld Patriarch" which the older writer wished to get back into print. He had published the original in 1910, and it had been "lost." Then again in 1931 he had regained this material as a short story in *The Secret Veld.* That too had been "lost." What he wished to reclaim was the story of a young man who with his hands killed a leopard that had made a fatal attack upon the girl he loved. In verse (1910) he had used seventy-five lines to present his story, but the 1931 prose narrative runs to fifteen pages set thirty-two lines to the page. In the prose form, he developed an elaborate "situation" into which the leopard-girl-man event is absorbed. The enveloping environment is competently handled, but the unframed incident as told by Oom Piet is no less effective, since the action carries its own climax and meaning.

What becomes most important in reading the prose version is that the details, which were few in the verse story, were expanded to give information which could only be conjectured in the short form. In "Veld Patriarch," Oom Piet becomes the structural center; Dirk and

the leopard are introduced in the second half. The short story, called
"Dirk's Dirge," presents Dirk before the character who takes Oom
Piet's place appears. A stranger, riding through East Griqualand,
finds himself at evening on the now steepening slopes beneath the
Drakensberg. He says this had happened about twenty years before
he related the events. It was something over twenty years earlier
that the young banker-author was sent to Matatiele, in East Griqualand. The house which the traveler sees in a "white-walled farm-
house," and three or four hundred yards beyond it, is the rocky
barrier dividing the lower from the upper slopes of the massive
range. This was to be the spot for the struggle between Dirk and the
leopard.

Everything suggests that as a young man Slater had come upon
this story during the almost ten years that he lived under the influence of the Drakensberg, and since that time it had held him in its
power. The story itself is elemental. Dirk is a man of complete and
direct simplicity, loving the natural world, especially the animals
that man has domesticated. When the girl, symbol of feminine
loveliness, appears, Dirk offers total devotion to this fragile creature.
Then one day at the gap in the rocky ridge up the mountains from
the house, the girl is attacked by a great leopard. Dirk, returning
home with the cattle, hears the human screams and rushes to the
spot. The girl lies torn and bloody. Dirk manages to get to the powerful animal and to obtain a grip on its throat. Though finally he
wins, the beloved one of his life is dead. Existence for Dirk continues, but the reason for life has been killed. Seemingly this story
and its relation to the old man of the veld symbolized something
very important to Slater, and for forty years he held tenaciously to
both.

Though the setting of "The Dead Eagle," which had not been
used in *Selected Poems*, suggests the Drakensberg, the human elements turn a reader toward Slater's literary orientation, which was
English. Here was the author's final attempt to project the essence
of the poetic life. His first recorded effort was made in "The Palace
of Poesy," written at the age of fourteen. His most extended attempt
was in the short story which in 1908 he called "Magic Casements"
and in its revised form "The Minstrel," 1931. As is true of almost
everything in this volume of "rejected" material, "The Dead Eagle"
was emotionally of profound importance to Slater. Initially his in-
volvement was with English poetry, and even in 1929 while writing

these lines he used an epigraph from Browning, a passage which
names Shelley. Yet, as was suggested in Chapter 13 (pp. 129-130).
Slater's subject seems to have grown with the years. Among other
things, the Olive Schreiner influence was interposed. Further association with South Africa came with the designating of a rising poet
of Natal as the young eagle. The final development was in the preparation of this volume for the press. Not only is the book dedicated
to General Smuts but is offered with these lines.

> Rarely, rarely may men render
> Witness to the grace and splendour
> Of the golden mountain-eagle,
> Bird of all earth's birds most regal,
> For to purblind human eyes
> He is but a moving shadow
> On the earth and in the skies.
>
> Eagle-beings who inherit
> High peaks of the human spirit,
> In their fastnesses are lonely,
> For their fellow-men see only
> Fitful hints of radiance thrown
> To the unremembering plains
> From Everests unknown.[4]

Resemblances between the dedication and the lines which were
to appear a few pages further into the book would seem too obvious
to assume that Slater did not know what he was doing. Not only the
poet but the statesman or any other great man sheds his influence
over the earth. The idea is ancient and common. Perhaps for this
reason Edmund Blunden dropped it from his selection. Slater had
returned it to a place among his important work because he *felt*
he had succeeded in reconstructing the idea from South African
materials.

To be placed with "Veld Patriarch" and "The Dead Eagle" as a
part of the author's life beyond any consideration of ideas and artistic power is "The Kloof." This had been written as late as 1931, but
it was concerned with early youth, with his dedication to poetry
when at the age of eight on the Slater farm he began to "Dream . . .
youth's incredible dreams."[5] In 1949 as he selected materials for
what seemed perhaps his last volume, he was loath to abandon

those dreams, especially since he now could believe that some of them were reality.

Though Slater's real reason for wanting this collection published was the deeply emotional attachment which has been traced in this chapter, the reason given the publisher had to be something more acceptable to the business world. This "business" reason was that he was offering material not yet published in book form. He could suggest the importance of "The Distraught Airman," which had been issued in a pamphlet to raise funds at the time of World War II. Among the new material is "Imilambo," packed with South African river names.

. . . softly-flowing Emthatha,
Known as Umtata and passing the tree-dappled town of that name;
Etsomo; Kutsolo or Hlokoma ("stream that rattles"):
Embage (Bashee); Enciba (Kei) whose mountainous banks
Divide the dwelling-places of the Dark People
From the land owned by the White: Egqhunube
Called by many the Gonubie: Enxaruni,
Now commonly called the Nahoon: Ekubuse ("at the honey")
So named because of its honey-sweet waters,
That flow near the twin-peaks, Amabele ("the breasts"),
Beautifully curved as those of a marriageable maiden:
Exesi (Keiskama), white stream flowing from the blue breast
Of Amatola ("the calves") Mountains and joined near Edikeni
(Alice) by Etyhume, which flows from Kwabelekusana
("At carrying babe on back") known as Hogsback Mountain. . . .[6]

Readers outside of South Africa will always be pleased to receive this type of material, for reasons which have nothing to do with literature. Most of them will be rather amazed to discover how much can be packed into so few lines.

IV Collected Poems

Having started with Blackwood in 1905, Francis Carey Slater ended with this publisher, in 1957, presenting *Collected Poems*. There would seem to be little doubt that this volume presents what the author wished to have known as his completed work. Appropriately, the volume starts with the *Dark Folk* pieces, twenty-eight being the final number. This was what his childhood on the farm had started preparing him to write. Second, there is the whole of

The Trek, history of his Afrikaans neighbors, whom he had known in childhood, just as he had known the Xhosa people. Then there is all of *Drought* and "The Karroo." Now at peace among the *Narrative, Historical, and Elegiac Poems* is "Veld Patriarch." With the lyrics is "The Dead Eagle" and "The Kloof." All that Slater wanted to save is present; all that he wished to revise has been put in a final form. Over the line into his eighties, he was permitted a last gathering and could now have literary peace.

Great satisfaction must have come to Slater from the preface which Roy Campbell wrote for *Collected Poems*. It was Campbell who with William Plomer and Laurens van der Post had brought South African literature to the attention of a world audience. Approval by the generation following him gave the ill but courageous old man the gift which he could value above all others. Very personal, Campbell's preface offered the right words with which to conclude his long career.

The Collected Poems of Francis Carey Slater span a period which was almost barren except for his own and the almost equally fine poetry of Arthur Shearly Cripps. I personally owe a great deal to their example for their talent blossomed without the encouragement with which South Africa so lavishly rewards her poets, especially those writing in Afrikaans to-day. Even I can still remember the time when "being a poet" incurred public hostility. The furore that greeted the publication of "Voorslag" by William Plomer, Laurens van der Post and myself was a healthy furore—a sign of South Africa's intellectual awakening. Such hostility is infinitely more encouraging than, and vastly preferable to, the long age of indifference and neglect which had to be weathered by Dr. Slater when he first acclimatised English poetry to these shores as the forerunner and pioneer of us all. His work has steadily developed in power, skill, range and variety. "The Dead Eagle" is as great as anything yet written by a South African. There is the widest variety between the terse, rough free-verse so aptly suited to "Drought" and the lyrical music of the "Dark Folk" series. His poetry ages like wine—inproving as he grows older. I am grateful for the honour of introducing this book since its publication is a great event in South African literature.[7]

Ironically, Roy Campbell died before Slater. Yet each had contributed that which would help South African literature to live and grow.

CHAPTER 16

Looking Back,
Settlers' Heritage, *1950-51*

D URING his middle seventies, Francis Carey Slater told the
story of his life in a book which he called *Settlers' Heritage*.
Here, both directly and indirectly, he revealed much that is important in a study of the man and his work. Throughout the account
a reader feels he is receiving Carey Slater as he was—not as he
wished the outside world to know him. Half of the volume had been
completed before in his narrative he reached the age of eighteen.
The second half took him from that period into his seventies.
Consideration of his own youth, or South Africa's youth, gave him
a chance to present the environment which he loved. Once this setting was completed, he had less to say than earlier.

When Slater turned his attention toward almost anything in or
about South Africa, his interest was immediately engaged. On the
first page of his autobiography, he commenced with comments
upon the 1820 Settlers, a natural beginning since on both sides he
was descended from them. Though he was proud of his 1820
ancestors, both generally and specifically, these men and women
were an important part of the history of the Cape, and mention of
them prompted him to offer detailed facts from much more than
a personal point of view. Crediting Lord Charles Somerset, governor
of the Cape of Good Hope, with attracting some five thousand settlers to South Africa through representations of the beauty, desirability, and potentialities of the land, he immediately explained the
governor's actual reason for wanting settlers.

Somerset's policy was well conceived, but badly executed. It was that of
protecting a frontier by close-settling farmers along it—an idea as old as
the Roman Empire in Europe, and often carried out there during the
Middle Ages. The Eastern frontier of the Cape Colony was at that time

greatly harassed by marauding bands from the region than known as Kaffirland. To combat these forays, the Governor planned to populate the land lying between the Bushman's River and the Great Fish River with British settlers, who would form a buffer between Kaffirland and the Cape Colony. The British Settlers of 1820, entirely unaware of the dangerous position in which they were to be placed, came from England in twenty-one sailing-ships, the first of which reached Algoa Bay on the 9th April, 1820. The other ships came in at intervals until the following June. The average time taken by the voyage from England was four months, so the settlers were sorely tried at the very outset of their great adventure.[1]

Despite all of the problems presented by an unfriendly population, soil unsuitable for many uses, lack of farming knowledge, strange wild animals, unfamiliar poisonous snakes, and severe droughts, the 1820 Settlers endured and finally in many ways built the country about which Somerset had fictionalized. Part of the proof of all of this was furnished by Slater's own family, and he wished to present their story.

I *Childhood and Maturity*

When young or when old, Slater was interested in any aspect of the history of South Africa, but he was always more deeply moved by his immediate environment than by anything in the past. His world was usually a very personal one. During the process of growing up in the Eastern Cape he had known much that was a part of the development of the country, and his individual experiences accurately reflect the general heritage. For instance, while presenting the neighborhood in which he lived as a child, he offered a paragraph on the introduction of wire fences into South Africa.

In the days of which I am writing there were no wire fences. The dividing fences between the various farms were made by chopping down thorn-trees and piling them tightly one upon the other. Our cattle-and-sheep-kraals were fenced in the same way. Not long after we went to Brakfontein I remember seeing one of the first wire-fences in the district put up between our own and a neighbour's farm. Shortly afterwards a friend, riding along a beaten-track to visit us, was amazed to find this unfamiliar barrier in his way, and was obliged to ride along the fence until he found entrance through a gate therein.[2]

An isolated recollection of this kind is trivial, but as one is added to another, on and on, a reader begins to develop a feeling for the country and for the period. At least one important aspect of this book, written in the 1950's, is that the South Africa of the author is already far, far away from the South Africa of the youth who encountered what is being depicted. Descriptions of normal work done in the late nineteenth century suggest much about the changes which had been made.

. . . In those days we used a single-furrow plough with a wooden frame, cast-iron furrower, and a steel share. Six or eight oxen, according to their size, were inspanned to draw the plough, and three persons—ploughman, driver and leader—were necessary for the operation of ploughing. At first I became a leader. Each of the front oxen had the end of a riem bound about its horns. The loose loop of the *riem,* thereby falling between the two oxen, was about the length of a child's skipping rope. The leader holds on to the middle of the loop, or *touw* as it is usually called, and guides the oxen along, with his back to them. The ox on his right, as he goes, should be kept walking along in the last ploughed furrow and its yoke-fellow on the unploughed ridge next to it. . . .

After serving my apprenticeship as a leader I was entrusted with a long whip and did the driving. This was an easy job, consisting mainly in ad-dressing individual oxen by name—sometimes with uncomplimentary addenda—and urging them on with occasional cracks of the whip or flicks on their broad backs. When I had grown sufficiently strong, I took over the ploughman's job. This I found harder but more interesting work than either leading or driving. When the field had been ploughed, my father, carrying the seed-wheat in a large apron tied to his waist, would walk up and down the field broadcasting the seed over the ploughed soil, and replenishing his apron-supply from sacks placed at each end of the field. Thereafter a harrow would be carefully drawn over the whole of the rough ploughed field.[3]

Despite the factual value of passages such as the account of plow-ing, nothing in it develops much to suggest that a human being is experiencing what is being described. Yet often there are sections in which young Francis is intensely present.

Children brought up on farms soon become accustomed to the sight of mating animals, and do not take much notice of such everyday occurrences. One afternoon I was sent to bring Helmet [a sixteen-hand stallion] home to his stable. When I neared him he was peacefully cropping the grass about a hundred yards from the Hoek fence. Just then three mares came in sight beyond the fence. Two of them were feeding as they moved slowly towards me. The third mare, evidently of a more amorous disposition than the others, came toward the fence emitting a gentle whinny of welcome. Helmet, with a series of fierce neighs, galloped towards her. He leaped lightly over the high wire-fence; and, making another leap, his great body curved splendidly into the shape of a sickle-blade. It was a sight of beauty and terror. I had never seen anything like it and, too terrified to go near the stallion and his mare, I immediately rushed home to tell my father. A Native servant was then sent for the valiant, high-flying Helmet.[4]

Looking back some fifty or sixty years, the now aging and unwell author remembered the work, the play, the events, the older people, and the places of his childhood. From him a reader learns many things about life in the Eastern Cape during the last quarter of the nineteenth century. It was his vocation which filled an important part of his mind. Though he made no such division, Slater might well have called the middle of his volume "The Making of a South African Career." As he moved from bank branch to bank branch, he was given a chance to know each village or town of South Africa to which his work sent him. Childhood had offered the story of life on an African farm, with its abounding open spaces. The middle years revealed an increasing concern for people, especially those his own age, and the many things which man has made, including a local war and then a world war. Slater never ceased to view with pleasure and sometimes awe the natural glories of South Africa, but it is man who increasingly demands his attention. Constant dealings with persons of all kinds was inevitable in any bank of this period, and the number of types encountered was increased by a system which continued to move a young man from one location to another.

II *As a Literary Critic*

While studying Francis Carey Slater, it is necessary to remember that from childhood to old age part of his mind was always focused on literature—regardless of where he was or what he was doing. Yet his autobiography demonstrates that he was almost totally incapable of discussing literature as literature—even his own books. The publication of his first volume elicited only a few sentences. Below is the total comment upon this event which, up to that time, must have been one of the most important of his life.

I wrote a fair number of poems, while I was at Matatiele, of which the two longest were "Footpaths Thro' the Veld" (free elegiacs) and "Lindani" (a narrative of Native life in blank verse). These and forty shorter poems (twenty of which had been written in my teens) I arranged in the order which seemed best and took with me in April 1905 when I left Matatiele for England, on long leave. I have long since realized how pitifully scanty was the grain in those youthful gleanings. Seven only of the original forty-two have been retained (four in revised form and three re-written) in my latest collections.[5]

If Slater's writing was important to him, and very definitely it was, why did he characterize it with statements such as "I have long since realized how pitifully scanty was the grain in those youthful gleanings"? The explanation for his procedure is probably very simple. His mind was essentially neither creative nor critical. Confronted with any need for evaluation, he turned to long exhausted metaphors. The irony here is worth noting: in the process of commenting upon literary weakness in youth, he was guilty of literary weakness in old age. Seemingly, he was unaware of his methods. Of his second book, short stories, he wrote that the narratives had been "simmering" in his mind; when written they were "christened" with a title and sent to a publisher.[6] In 1924 when he said he discovered how poor his writing was he confessed that he had been previously "playing at poetry instead of sweating at it."[7] Even when he essayed to discuss the arrangement of the forty-two pieces in his first volume ("arranged in the order which seemed best"),[8] he appears not to notice that his explanation does not explain. His statement probably was intended to imply that the order was not chronological, but what type of sequence was used is never indicated. Nor is it possible to suggest that he was writing for those who in the 1950's, either inside or outside of South Africa, would have known the order used in a volume published almost half a century earlier. Regardless of where a student probes into passages of this kind, he is forced to the conclusion that the author simply was without an analytical mind.

Once in his autobiography, he did discuss at length a single volume, *Drought*, written in 1928 and published in 1929 under the name of Jan Van Avond. Here he devoted some two thousand words to what he had written twenty-three years earlier. Almost exactly half of his space is used for a prose summary because he felt that few had read in verse what he had said. The second half of his consideration is an examination of the politics of South Africa. At the proper place in the autobiography he had noted the publication of *Drought* and observed that he had "decided to try [his] hand at free verse."[9] He stated that "In England the book was noticed and commended by all the leading newspapers and reviews. In South Africa it enjoyed a mixed reception: some of the newspapers praised it, but several others doubted whether '*Drought* could be called poetry at all!' "[10] Slater's treatment of *Drought* gives additional emphasis to the claim that searching for literary criticism here is quite useless. Little will be found.

III   *Recording of Trips*

Another area of the story of his life which reveals something significant about the author is the relative weight given two trips that he took after retirement. A 1933 visit to Southern Rhodesia is presented in thirteen words. The next year a vacation in England and on the Continent received more than a hundred times this number of words. Various emphases are to be expected, but the range here is great enough to deserve the designation of "fantastic." It seems reasonable to assume that Slater is revealing unconscious value judgments in this vast discrepancy. Africa he loved, but almost without exception this meant his own Africa, the Cape Province. England and Europe, however, were for him things of the spirit. Their architecture, art, music, literature, and related aspects had been from childhood literally worshiped. When he saw these places, he felt himself to be in a sacred environment of one kind or another. The places he visited had long ago become symbols of a poet and his writing, a composer and his operas—the creator and what he had created. One of Slater's aims in life was to give South Africa, for example, a literature because he felt there was all too little that was as yet of value. A basic reason for the difference was that South African poetry in English had existed only a hundred years, whereas England could look back upon a thousand years and parts of Europe more than two thousand years. In one sense Slater was a victim of an aspect of history.

Perhaps something of how Slater felt about what he was to see, or at least wanted to see in England and Europe may be observed in an incident which happened upon his initial visit in 1905. It was his first morning in Paris, and he had gone to the Louvre. As he approached the building, he reports that he observed guides "parading before it like eager racehorses." One speaks to him in English, and here the story takes an unexpected direction.

> . . . I stared at him vacantly, and he readily switched over into two or three other languages. Finally I looked him firmly in the face and said solemnly: *"Eqaqa liya ziqika qika kuqaqaqa laqhawuka uqhoqhoqho"* (A Xhosa sentence devised to exhibit certain clicks peculiar to Bantu languages). This was too much for him, and he went on his way—not rejoicing, but probably wondering what specimen of the ape species he had encountered. I was then free to spend a happy day in the Louvre . . . .[11]

Though most of Slater's characteristics suggest a predictable man, the above incident was certainly not quite anticipated. Then, too, occasionally he slipped into his narrative something that a reader is not likely to expect or forget. Near the time of Dr. James Stewart's death, young Francis was making what was to be his last visit to the now ill doctor. Slater reported that the old missionary quite calmly told him that he was near death. It was not death that was on his mind, but the future of England. He predicted that the downfall of England would be effected by Kaiser Wilhelm II or the Labour party. This was 1905.[12]

IV *What He Needed from the Bank*

Certainly one of the actions of Francis Carey Slater that could be predicted is that despite his longing to be an author, especially a poet, he would remain with the Standard Bank until time for retirement. The question was raised more than once, the last time he reports was in 1910, while he was at Somerset East. His second book, a collection of stories called *The Sunburnt South*, had been read by the manager under whom he was then working. The manager had said that he could not understand why a person of his talents remained in the bank. The already published author knew very well why he remained. At this particular place in the story he remarks upon the uncertainty of a literary career. Elsewhere he gives a more solid reason, one to which there was no reply. South Africa offered no market. When Slater was making his reply to the complimentary manager, the English population of his country was only slightly more than half a million. Even if an author could produce a successful book every few years (or even every year), it would be impossible to live on the basis of an income derived from serious writing. Another fact which the new accountant did not report being discussed was that he was planning to be married soon and would need a larger rather than smaller (not to say uncertain) income. Regardless of the reasons given or not given in the conversation, he remained with the bank and permitted his literary development to move very slowy.

V   *Slater and Smuts*

How tenaciously Slater clung to his concepts of what literature could do can be seen in his indicating a parallel between himself and General Smuts. Early in the autobiography, he mentions that at six he was engaged in the herding of sheep. Then he adds that at about the same time a boy of twelve was herding sheep among the hills of the Malmesbury district. This other boy was also reading Shelley as he tended his father's sheep. The second boy was Jan Christiaan Smuts, with whose name Slater ended his book and with whom he corresponded for many years when they were both older men. Slater considered General Smuts the greatest of South Africa's statesmen of the century. There was no doubt in Slater's mind that a connection existed between the human potential with which Smuts started, a boy's work upon the veld under a burning sun, and the reading of great poetry. Though he was under no false conception as to the relationship between General Smuts and himself, he was aware of the parallels. He too had known the veld and the sun and the great poetry—and for all of the rest he hoped. One thing is certain: he seems to have appreciated profoundly the attention given him by General Smuts, who assured him that one of the lyrics in *The Trek* "is a chant not merely to Retief but to the Spirit of Leadership which rises like a flame above the drab level of our commonplaceness. It catches the very essence of what is great in our story."[13] Some years later Smuts was writing him that his work in general offered "Something of the intimate spirit of South Africa" which now is given to the world in an edition from Oxford and could "be enjoyed by those who do not know the South Africa which is ours."[14]

CHAPTER 17

Conclusion

A MONG the pioneer group which in 1820 had sought for various reasons the South African sun was Thomas Pringle, a
young Scot already possessing a European education and some
reputation as a poet. Despite a verse style unsuited to his new situation, he was able to record reactions to this strange environment.
Both Pringle's South African sojourn and his life were brief, but he
resided in the Cape long enough to create a body of work around
which other writers might gather for many years after his death.
There would come a time, however, when Thomas Pringle no longer
exerted a germinal force. As he receded into history, either someone
or something would be required to fill what must otherwise have
resulted in a vacuum.

Long before "the father of South African poetry in English"
slipped back into history, the something which was to take his place
had commenced to form. The "something" was a love for South
Africa. Love was first manifested as an artistic impulse in isolated
expressions because the process of settling a new country left little
time for literary development. The desperate exigencies of main-
taining protection against various destructive forces, of erecting
buildings in which to live, and of providing food required most of
the available hours of men, women, and children. Even the most
elementary formal academic training was often in abeyance. Under
these conditions artistic creation was forgotten, ignored, or left to
the future.

That future, however, was to be at least partially realized in the
life and writing of Francis Carey Slater, whose maturing was as
natural as that of a tree planted by the English pioneers in the Eastern Cape. Slater was the fourth generation of his family to live in
South Africa but only the second to be born there. In his time it was
possible to emerge from the soil of the country and absorb into one's
being all of the fundamental elements of the environment. When

165

he came to maturity, he was prepared to present to his country
something it needed but did not yet know it wanted.

What South Africa needed, what any country needs, was the
perspective with which to evaluate itself—not too much acceptance,
but not too little. Human imperfection guarantees that the task will
never end, but much virtue may be found in an honest and vigor-
ous attempt. Credit must be given Francis Carey Slater for all that
he initiated and for the distance he carried his country from the
various points of inception.

Perhaps the first contribution which Slater made to South Africa
was the extensive work he did in making books available to those
who otherwise would have gone without reading material. In a
new and isolated land, adequate private libraries are certain to be
rare. When Slater was young not even many public libraries de-
served the name. He worked hard and systematically to improve
conditions, and town after town saw the effect of his residence,
brief though it often was in the early years.

Through his own life, this banker-author encouraged his country
to believe that there was no conflict between business and the arts.
As a banker, he was devoted to his work, but he was also by practice
a defender of literature. His first book was published when he had
been with the bank only long enough to merit his initial long leave.
Between this time and retirement, he published nine additional
volumes. To his associates, he was a constant reminder of a business-
man who could write, or of a writer who could succeed in the world
of business. After what must be thought of as his apprentice years,
to both business and literature, Slater seems to have been honored
for both his banking and his writing as he moved from one assignment to another.

Slowly, as book followed book Slater the author came to understand that literature is here and now, not yonder and long ago. Very
early he employed South African materials, but only gradually was
he to understand how to use what he held very close to him. In the
beginning, his forms, diction, and attitude derived from literature
of the past which was also thousands of miles distant. At best, imi-
tation of such writing creates the incongruous; at its worst, the
pathetic. During the 1920's Slater noticed what he was doing and
began to comprehend something of what would be required of him
if he were to attain the goal which for many years he had sought.

Noticing the natural facts of a country, whether admiring or condemning them, will never produce literature of more than an elementary kind or mediocre quality. A writer must people his landscape. Reality emanates from life being lived. Slater seems to have stumbled upon this simple fact, without quite understanding it, when he began to write of the Xhosa people who had been a part of his experience from prerational years. As he wrote about these red blanket people, he made them a part of the landscape and it was a part of them. The author did what was right because it was actual, not because he grasped the literary principle involved. One assumes, however, that before he made his final revisions and arrangements of the "Dark Folk" materials he had come to a considerable degree of comprehension of why he was right.

More slowly but upon much the same principle, he learned to fit The Afrikaans people into their natural environment. In *The Trek*, setting, characters, action, and images merge. The Drakensberg do not here, as elsewhere, offer awe-inspiring scenery but terrain which creates an all but impossible descent for wagons moving down into the Promised Land of Natal. When the trekkers finally reach Natal, the land does not offer waving grass but waving spears which bring destruction and death to many. If the result is not great writing, at least the methods upon which this kind of writing must depend have been found.

Mastery of self and the present is always the most difficult task man can be given, in life or in literature. It was in *Drought* that Slater attempted to solve the problem of himself as author, the English from whom he was descended and their relation to the Afrikaans and Bantu peoples (and the relation of each to the other two), and current problems of the civilization in which he lived. It was in trying to write *Drought* that he began to learn in a very serious way the relationship between form and the total impact of a literary effort. In *Drought* he struggled with diction, imagery, versification, narration, and organization as in none of his previous work. Significantly those parts of *Drought* are most successful where he has created esthetic distance through mastery of technique. As usual, the principles involved are very simple. For example, an image has more universal emotional appeal than an abstract statement; action generates more impact than description; any method of accretion or accumulation moves to a climax in a way which no quantity of ideological claims can ever reach. All of these principles may be found operating in the composition of *The Trek*.

Evidence that Slater was developing an understanding of the basic methods of literature is also indicated by the fact that at the time of the composition of *Drought* he was writing his best short stories, and revising the early stories for inclusion in a collection called *The Secret Veld*.[1] Perhaps it is not quite idle to speculate as to what might have happened if he had been able to devote more time to short prose fiction. Because he considered it a less exalted literary form, he might have been able to relax enough to make promising stories into something quite good. He convinced himself, however, that brief fictional work would do little for him economically (the reason he gave for writing it at this time) and perhaps even less for his reputation. Thus he abandoned the short-story form for the rest of his writing life.

Whatever one decides about Slater's rejection of prose fiction after he had published a novel in 1925 and written a number of new stories in 1926-27, the period from 1924 to 1927 revealed continuous internal struggle. It was in 1924 that he admitted to himself something which required courage to accept. He came to understand that the verse he had been publishing for some twenty years was not writing in which he could feel justifiable pride, was not even anything he wished to preserve. Subsequent events proved that he was absolutely correct in his assessment. His reputation when he died in 1958 was built almost totally upon what he did after 1924. Everything before that date could have been destroyed without damage to the position he was to hold in South African literature.

After the publication in 1924 of *The Karroo*, Slater began to press so hard that he came very close to the point of destroying his health. During 1924 he pushed himself to the completion of his long contemplated collection of South African verse in English. At the same time he was writing a novel. He saw both through the press while he was in England in 1925. Back in South Africa he began to write short stories, 1926-27. During the next year an actual drought and a particular political situation precipitated an experiment in verse from which he never returned to prose. Because what he started writing was to be published without any suggestion of the author's identity, for the first time in his life Slater seems to have felt free to attempt anything he wished. *Drought* quickly became the beginning of a career, not the end of one. Nor did he have long to wait before he could claim what was his own, for only two years remained until retirement made possible his designation as the author.

Many or even most young writers who were beginning to publish in the 1920's appear to have looked upon Slater as a writer of the past. Roy Campbell speaks for the group when he says, "My first impression of *Drought* was that it was the work of a young man, simply because it is frank, outspoken and highspirited."[2] Campbell made this statement after learning the authorship. His words show very simply that he considered the characteristics named as the possession of his own generation, not the writers of Slater's age, a man now into his fifties. Young Roy was wrong. The older man had grown slowly, but he had continued to grow.

Beginning to impinge upon him first when he was fourteen and still present when he wrote an autobiography during his middle seventies, the persistent problem of Francis Carey Slater's life was the one of finding ways to depict the South Africa which he saw around him and of making into literature what he felt was within him to be said. South Africa pervaded his being as completely as the blood which flowed through his body. In youth something within urged him to make poems about South Africa. His intention had been completely clear in "Footpaths Thro' the Veld," written before 1905. Yet the young author's language was inadequate for his undertaking. The mistake he made is a usual one. Often a youthful reader assumes the language of an individual poem, author, or period and place is the language of poetry in a universal sense. When as a boy Slater read the English Romantic poets, he accepted them as poetry, not merely as poets of one time, place, and literary style. In other circumstances this error might have been educated out of him in a normal way. Because this was not possible, he was left to learn painfully as a mature man that he held the attitude of a literary adolescent. Yet one must stand in admiration at the courage which was required to begin after the age of fifty to create the literary reputation for which he had longed profoundly since fourteen. Not only did he secure much of the success for which he had lived but he earned the gratitude of many in a country which had not sought his leadership. Finally, however, some recognized that almost alone he had furnished the substance for the growing period between the pioneering sowers and the mid-twentieth-century harvesters.

Notes and References

Chapter One

1. Information for this chapter has been drawn from *Settlers' Heritage*, Francis Carey Slater, published by the Lovedale Press, Alice, Cape Province, South Africa, 1954.
2. Slater, *Settlers' Heritage*, p. 57.
3. *Ibid.*, p. 98.
4. *Ibid.*, pp. 114-116.

Chapter Two

1. Slater, *Settlers' Heritage*, p. 1.
2. Francis Carey Slater, *Footpaths Thro' the Veld and Other Songs and Idylls of South Africa* (Cape Town, Edinburgh, and London, 1905), pp. 85-86.
3. *Settlers' Heritage*, pp. 175-76.
4. *Times* (London), December, 1905.
5. Slater, *Footpaths Thro' the Veld*, pp. 1-2.
6. *Times* (London), December, 1905.
7. *Settlers' Heritage*, p. 123.
8. *Footpaths Thro' the Veld*, pp. 50-51.
9. *Ibid.*, p. 17.
10. *Ibid.*, pp. 22-23.

Chapter Three

1. Francis Carey Slater, *The Sunburnt South* (London, 1908), p. 35.
2. Slater, *Footpaths Thro' the Veld*, p. 86.
3. Olive Schreiner, *The Story of an African Farm*, 1883.
4. Slater, *The Sunburnt South*, p. 167.
5. *Ibid.*, pp. 11-12.
6. *Ibid.*, pp. 26-27.
7. *Ibid.*, pp. 71-72.

Chapter Four

1. Slater, *Footpaths Thro' the Veld*, p. 102.
2. Francis Carey Slater, *Collected Poems* (Edinburgh, London, and Johannesburg-Cape Town, 1957), p. 313.

3. *Ibid.*, p. 314 or *From Mimosa Land*, p. 18.
4. Francis Carey Slater, *From Mimosa Land* (Edinburgh and London, 1910), p. 19.
5. *Ibid.*, pp. 80-82.
6. *Ibid.*, p. 89.
7. *Ibid.*, p.92

Chapter Five

1. Slater, *Settlers' Heritage*, p. 200.
2. *Ibid.*, p. 201.
3. Francis Carey Slater, *Calls Across the Sea* (Edinburgh and London, 1916), p. 15.
4. *Ibid.*, p. 23.
5. *Ibid.*, p. 17.
6. *Ibid.*, p. 24.
7. *Ibid.*, p. 32.
8. *Ibid.*, p. 16.
9. *Ibid.*, p. 35.

Chapter Six

1. Slater, *Settlers' Heritage*, p. 205.
2. Francis Carey Slater, *Settlers and Sunbirds* (Edinburgh and London, 1919), pp. 20-21.
3. *Ibid.*, p. 41.

Chapter Seven

1. Slater, *Settlers' Heritage*, p. 206.
2. Francis Carey Slater, *The Karroo and Other Poems* (Edinburgh and London, 1924), pp. 13-29.
3. *Ibid.*, p. 40.
4. *Ibid.*, pp. 13-15.
5. *Ibid.*, p. 20.
6. *Ibid.*, p. 21.
7. *The Lost World of the Kalahari.*
8. Slater, *The Karroo and Other Poems*, p. 24.
9. *Ibid.*, pp. 24-25.
10. Slater, *The Sunburnt South*, p. 73.
11. *The Karroo and Other Poems*, pp. 11-29.
12. *Ibid.*, pp. 54-55.

Chapter Eight

1. Indebted to a line by William Plomer.
2. *New York Times*, Dec. 13, 1925, p. 8.
3. Francis Carey Slater, *The Shining River* (London, New York, Toronto, Bombay, Calcutta, and Madras, 1925), p. 8.
4. *Ibid.*, p. 7.
5. *Ibid.*, p. 3.
6. *Ibid.*, p. 36.
7. *Ibid.*, p. 34.
8. *Ibid.*, pp. 6-7.
9. *Ibid.*, p. 7.
10. *Ibid.*, pp. 143-144.
11. *Ibid.*, p. 144 and p. 305.
12. *Ibid.*, p. 109.
13. *Ibid.*
14. *Ibid.*, p. 44.

Chapter Nine

1. Slater, *Settlers' Heritage*, p. 110.
2. Francis Carey Slater, editor, *The Centenary Book of South African Verse* (London, New York, Toronto, Bombay, Calcutta, and Madras, 1925), pp. vii-x.
3. *Ibid.*, p. 160.
4. *Ibid.*, p. 200.
5. *Ibid.*, p. 75.
6. *Ibid.*, p. 59.
7. *Ibid.*, p. 222.

Chapter Ten

1. Slater, *Settlers' Heritage*, pp. 224-29.
2. Francis Carey Slater, *Drought* (London, 1929), p. 11.
3. *Ibid.*, p. 12.
4. *Ibid.*, p. 17.
5. *Ibid.*, p. 18.
6. *Ibid.*, p. 22 and p. 24.
7. *Ibid.*, p. 40.
8. *Ibid.*
9. *Ibid.*, p. 45.
10. *Ibid.*, p. 49.
11. *Ibid.*, p. 48.
12. *Ibid.*, p. 50.
13. *Ibid.*, p. 55.

14. *Ibid.*, p. 63.
15. Dustjacket to *Dark Folk*.
16. *Settlers' Heritage*, p. 261.
17. *Ibid.*, p. 259.
18. *Ibid.*, p. 256.
19. *Ibid.*, p. 258.
20. Slater, *Drought*, p. 34.
21. *Ibid.*, p. 38.
22. *Ibid.*, p. 56.
23. *Ibid.*, p. 22.
24. *Ibid.*, p. 11.
25. *Ibid.*, p. 46.
26. *Ibid.*, p. 47.
27. *Ibid.*, p. 49.
28. *Ibid.*, p. 64.

Chapter Eleven

1. Slater, *Settlers' Heritage*, pp. 209-11.
2. Slater, *Collected Poems*, pp. 256-57.
3. *Ibid.*, p. 240.
4. *Settlers' Heritage*, pp. 214-15.
5. G. M. Miller and Howard Sergeant, *A Critical Survey of South African Poetry in English* (Cape Town and Amsterdam, 1957), p. 75.
6. *Ibid.*
7. *Ibid.*, p. 71.

Chapter Twelve

1. Francis Carey Slater, *The Secret Veld* (London, 1931), pp. 9-11.
2. Slater, *Settlers' Heritage*, p. 86.
3. Slater, *The Secret Veld*, p. 93.
4. *Ibid.*, pp. 19-20.
5. *Ibid.*, pp. 20-21.
6. *Ibid.*, pp. 59-60.
7. *Ibid.*, p. 61.
8. *Ibid.*, p. 69.
9. *Ibid.*, pp. 70-71.
10. *Ibid.*, pp. 72-73.
11. *Ibid.*, p. 74.
12. Robert Penn Warren, "The Ballad of Billie Potts."
13. *The Secret Veld*, p. 195.

Chapter Thirteen

1. Francis Carey Slater, *Dark Folk and Other Poems* (Edinburgh and London, 1935), p. 22.
2. *Ibid.*, p. 29.
3. *Ibid.*, p. 30.
4. *Ibid.*, pp. 30-31.
5. *Ibid.*, p. 3.
6. *Ibid.*, pp. 33-34.
7. *Ibid.*, pp. 24-25.
8. *Ibid.*, p. 57.
9. *Ibid.*, p. 58.
10. *Ibid.*, p. 59.
11. *Ibid.*, p. 60.
12. Slater, *Settlers' Heritage*, p. 3.
13. Slater, *Dark Folk and Other Poems*, p. 85.
14. *Ibid.*, p. 54.
15. *Ibid.*, p. 71.
16. *Ibid.*, p. 84.
17. *Ibid.*, p. 83.
18. *Ibid.*
19. *Ibid.*
20. *Ibid.*, p. 84.
21. *Ibid.*
22. *Ibid.*, p. 83.

Chapter Fourteen

1. Francis Carey Slater, *The Trek* (London, 1938), p. 21.
2. *Ibid.*, p. 34.
3. *Ibid.*, pp. 35-36.
4. *Ibid.*, p. 42.
5. *Ibid.*, p. 51.
6. *Ibid.*, p. 53.
7. *Ibid.*, pp. 94-95.
8. *Ibid.*, pp. 104-5.
9. *Ibid.*, p. 119.
10. *Ibid.*, p. 125.
11. *Ibid.*, p. 127.
12. *Ibid.*, p. 146.
13. *Ibid.*, pp. 146-47.
14. *Ibid.*, p. 101.
15. *Ibid.*, p. 102.
16. *Ibid.*, p. 111.
17. *Ibid.*, p. 113.

18. *Ibid.*, pp. 86-87.
19. *Ibid.*, p. 89.
20. *Ibid.*, p. 42.
21. *Ibid.*, p. 78.
22. *Ibid.*, p. 84.
23. *Ibid.*, p. 66.
24. *Ibid.*, p. 152.
25. *Ibid.*, pp. 155-56.

Chapter Fifteen

1. Letter from E. C. K. Ensor, *The Beacon*, High Wycombe, High Wyc. 350, Bucks., December 28, 1938, to Frank Nutt. The letter is in the possession of the author of this volume.
2. Francis Carey Slater, *Veld Patriarch and Other Poems* (London, New York, and Toronto, 1949), p. 1.
3. Slater, *Settlers' Heritage*, p. 157.
4. Slater, *Veld Patriarch and Other Poems*, p. v.
5. *Ibid.*, p. 11.
6. *Ibid.*, p. 25.
7. Slater, *Collected Poems*, p. vii.

Chapter Sixteen

1. Slater, *Settlers' Heritage*, pp. 1-2.
2. *Ibid.*, p. 10.
3. *Ibid.*, pp. 55-56.
4. *Ibid.*, pp. 46-47.
5. *Ibid.*, pp. 175-76.
6. *Ibid.*, p. 192.
7. *Ibid.*, p. 206.
8. *Ibid.*, p. 175.
9. *Ibid.*, p. 207.
10. *Ibid.*, pp. 207-8.
11. *Ibid.*, p. 185.
12. *Ibid.*, p. 186.
13. *Ibid.*, p. 233.
14. *Ibid.*, p. 240.

Chapter Seventeen

1. Stories written in 1926-27, see page 105, and published in 1931 as *The Secret Veld*.
2. Slater, *Settlers' Heritage*, p. 256.

Selected Bibliography

PRIMARY SOURCES

Footpaths Thro' the Veld and Other Songs and Idylls of South Africa.
Edinburgh and London: Blackwood, and Cape Town: Maskew Miller,
1905.

The Sunburnt South. London: Digby, Long, 1908.

From Mimosa Land. Edinburgh and London: Blackwood, 1910.

Calls Across the Sea. Edinburgh and London: Blackwood, 1917.

Settlers and Sunbirds. Edinburgh and London: Blackwood, 1919.

The Karroo and Other Poems. Edinburgh and London: Blackwood, 1924.

The Centenary Book of South African Verse, Chosen and Arranged by
Francis Carey Slater. London, New York, Toronto, Bombay, Calcutta,
and Madras: Longmans, Green, 1925.

The Shining River. London, New York, Toronto, Bombay, Calcutta, and
Madras: Longmans, Green, 1925.

Drought: A South African Parable, by Jan Van Avond [pseudonym].
London: Benn, 1929.

The Secret Veld. London: Nash & Grayson, 1931.

"*Zambesi*," with photographs by Telfer Shiel. Wynberg: Speciality Press,
[1934?]

Dark Folk and Other Poems. Edinburgh and London: Blackwood, 1935.

The Trek. London: Macmillan, 1938.

The Distraught Airman and Other Wartime Verses. [Wynberg: Rustica
Press, 1942?]

The New Century Book of South African Verse, Chosen and Arranged by
Francis Carey Slater. London, New York, Toronto: Longmans, Green,
1945.

Selected Poems of Francis Carey Slater. London: Oxford, 1947.

Veld Patriarch and Other Poems. London, New York, Toronto: Longmans,
Green, 1949.

Settlers' Heritage. Lovedale, C. P., South Africa: The Lovedale Press,
1954.

Collected Poems of Francis Carey Slater. Edinburgh and London: Blackwood, and Cape Town: Central News Agency, 1957.

SECONDARY SOURCES

Biography and Criticism

"Banker: D.Litt." *South African Banker,* 44: 301-2, January, 1948.

Recognition by a business periodical of an honorary degree in literature awarded to one of its men.

BUTLER, GUY. "South African Poetry in English," *The Concise Encyclopedia of English and American Poetry*, edited by Stephen Spender and Donald Hall. London: Hutchinson, 1963, p. 314. One of the few listings in an international context.

————. *A Book of South African Verse*, selected and introduced by Guy Butler, London: Oxford University Press, 1959, p. xxxi. In his introduction Butler claims that Slater was "the first South African to write poetry, not verse."

"Death of Dr. Francis Carey Slater." *South African Outlook*, 88:155, October, 1958. One of the comments upon Slater at the time of his death.

DELIUS, ANTHONY R. "Tribute to a Pioneer of English Poetry in South Africa," *Evening Post*, September 20, 1958. This appeared something over two weeks after Slater's death and was written by one of South Africa's best poets.

"Dr. F. C. Slater." *The Friend*, June 17, 1957. Appeared during the period which saw the publication of *Collected Poems*, the final work of the author's life.

"Dr. Francis Carey, Slater." *The Friend*, February 15, 1954. Coinciding with the year of publication of Slater's autobiography, the last book he wrote.

DODD, A. D. *Anthology of Short Stories by South-African Writers*, selected by A. D. Dodd, Cape Town: Juta, 1938 (?), p. 212. Brief attention given Slater's short prose fiction.

"Doyen of Union's 'English' Poets Dies in City," *Cape Times*, September 3, 1958. Notice of Slater's death.

"Eighty-Two-Year-Old Poet Loves His Country." *Cape Argus*, September 3, 1958. Immediate recognition upon Slater's death of one of his most important characteristics.

HARHOFF, THEODORE JOHANNES. "South African Poetry," *Encyclopedia of Poetry and Poetics*, edited by Alex Preminger. Princeton University Press, 1965, p. 791. An American listing.

HARVEY, C. J. D. " 'Local Colour' in South African Poetry," *Theoria*, 7:94-95, 1955. One of the few studies of Slater presented by a university magazine.

"He Sought for South Africa." *Cape Argus*, September 6, 1958. Emphasis upon a salient characteristic a few days after Slater's death.

"Honour for a South African Poet." *South African Outlook*, 78: 93-95, June, 1948. A brief evaluation near the end of his active career.

MACNAB, ROY with GULSTON, CHARLES. *South African Poetry*; a new anthology . . . with a foreward by Roy Campbell. London: Collins, 1948,

178 FRANCIS CAREY SLATER

pp. xxi-xxiii. Roy Campbell's foreward contains references to Slater, who was omitted from the anthology. In 1958 Roy MacNab included Slater in his anthology called *Poets in South Africa*.

MILLER, G. M. and SERGEANT, HOWARD. *A Critical Survey of South African Poetry in English*. Cape Town: Balkema, 1957, pp. 11, 12, 17, 34, 36, 46, 55, 60, 62, 63, 66, 84-100, 105, 106, 111, 116, 149. This is the most complete study, in book form, of Slater up to this time, the year before his death, and places him within the general South African context. These author's have written an assessment that will stand as the beginning of Slater criticism within a bound volume.

MITFORD-BARBERTON, IVAN, and WHITE, VIOLET. *Some Frontier Families*, biographical sketches of 100 Eastern Province families before 1840. Cape Town: Human & Rousseau, 1968, p. 255. Historical and geographical placing of the Slater family.

Natal Who's Who. Durban: Natal Who's Who Publishing Co., 1906, p, 181. Early recognition.

NATHAN, MANFRED. *South African Literature*. Cape Town: Juta, 1957, p, 183. Brief mention in a history of the literature of his country.

"Our Banker Poet, an Appreciation of Francis Carey Slater." *South African Banker*, 55: 227-28, September, 1958. A tribute from the business world at the time of his death.

"Our Pioneer Poet." *The Friend*, September 6, 1958. Emphasis upon Slater the forerunner, published the week of his death.

"Resurgamus." (Editorial) *South African P.E.N. Yearbook*. Johannesburg: 1960, p. 7. This page is a tribute to Slater, who was president of PEN from 1947 to 1958. The issue is dedicated to Slater's memory.

ROSE, BRIAN. "Fifty Years of South African Verse," *South African P.E.N. Yearbook*. Johannesburg: 1960, pp. 18, 19, 20, 21. The treatment here is completely sympathetic to Slater, which should be expected in a volume presented in his memory.

———. "Francis Carey Slater: A Tribute," *South African P.E.N. Yearbook*. Johannesburg: 1960, pp. 97-99. Despite the restrictions under which the author was working (publishing in a memorial volume), a reader feels that what he says is relevant—as well as deeply felt.

———. "Roy Campbell: A Tribute." *South African P.E.N. Yearbook*. Cape Town: 1956-57, p. 28. Roy Campbell, twenty-five years Slater's junior, was dead at fifty-six. He had just before his death written a preface to Slater's *Collected Poems*, 1957.

ROSENTHAL, ERIC. *Southern African Dictionary of National Biography*. London: Warne, 1966, p. 345. Another international listing.

SEARY, E. R. *A Biographical and Bibliographical Record of South African Literature*. Grahamstown: tentative edition, 1938, p. 52.

SNYMAN, J. P. L. "The South African Novel in English (1880-1930)." Potchefstroom University, 1952, p. 159, footnotes 1 and 2; and p. 182. The lack of discussion of his novel suggests the place Slater holds in this literary form.

SPEIGHT, W. L. "South African Poetry," *Empire Review and Magazine*, 57: 39-44, January, 1933, p. 40 and p. 43. References in a brief article.

THOMPSON, Miss E. M. *A South African Literary Reader*. Cape Town and Johannesburg: Juta, 1926, p. 223. Representation on the basis of the work of the first half of his career.

VARLEY, D. H. "Carey Slater as Digter." *Die Burger*, September 9, 1958. Notice by the Afrikaans press at the time of Slater's death. Written by the Chief Librarian of the South African Library.

WALKER, OLIVER. "Literature Honours Banker-Poet." *South African Banker*, 47: 297-99, November, 1950.

WEBSTER, MARY MORISON. "Francis Carey Slater, A Critical Comment," *South African P.E.N. Yearbook* Johannesburg: 1960, pp. 27-30. An assessment by one of the most respected poets of South Africa, who claims "that it was largely through his [Slater's] efforts that English verse in this country attained its present stature and prestige."

Reviews

Footpaths Thro' the Veld: Times Literary Supplement, December 8, 1905.

The Sunburnt South: Times Literary Supplement, January 17, 1909.

From Mimosa Land: Times Literary Supplement, December 15, 1910.

Calls Across the Sea: Times Literary Supplement, March 1, 1917.

The Karroo and Other Poems: South African Outlook, 55: 47, February, 1925.

The Shining River: Voorslag, December, 1926.

The Centenary Book of South African Verse: Times Literary Supplement, February 25, 1926.

Drought: Times Literary Supplement, June 20, 1929.

The Secret Veld: Times Literary Supplement, October 1, 1931.

Zambesi: South African Outlook, 64: 38-39, February, 1934.

Dark Folk and Other Poems: Critic IV (2): 117-18 (by W. S. Mackie), February, 1936.

The Trek: Times Literary Supplement, December 17, 1938.

The Distraught Airman and Other Wartime Verses: South African Outlook, 72: 191, November, 1942.

The New Centenary Book of South African Verse: South African Outlook, 75: 122-23, August, 1945.

Selected Poems of Francis Carey Slater: British Africa Monthly, March, 1948. (by Roy Campbell)

Veld Patriarch and Other Poems: South African Outlook, 79: 142, September, 1949.

Settlers' Heritage: Times Literary Supplement, April 23, 1954.

Collected Poems of Francis Carey Slater: English Studies in Africa, 2: 148-49, March, 1959. (by A. C. Partridge)

Index